Keep 'em Reading

CROSSWORD PUZZLES

101 Fun and Challenging Puzzles

Marguerite D. Lewis

UpstartBooks

Fort Atkinson, Wisconsin

To my granddaughters Rebecca and Amanda, that their inherent love for books and reading along with their thirst for knowledge will enrich and reward them all their lives.

Published by **UpstartBooks**
W5527 Highway 106
P.O. Box 800
Fort Atkinson, Wisconsin 53538-0800
1-800-448-4887

© Marguerite D. Lewis, 2004

The paper used in this publication meets the minimum requirements of American National Standard for Information Science—Permanence of Paper for Printed Library Material. ANSI/NISO Z39.48-1992.

Contents

Introduction

Students love crossword puzzles. They think of them as a challenge, pitting their knowledge against those neat little squares, just begging to be filled in. Fun aside, crossword puzzles are an excellent tool for review, reinforcement, retention and sequence of literature. Even with Whole Language on the wane, teachers and librarians know the value of students being able to select their own books for reading as an enrichment to phonics and commercial reading programs.

Teachers and librarians are busy. They don't always have the time to check the knowledge and understanding of the titles students independently select and read. As students complete the puzzles in this book, you can gauge your students' knowledge and understanding of the stories.

The reading skills of students in grades K–3 varies greatly. Therefore, the selection of titles in this resource includes picture books, which can be read to or by the student, beginning to advance "I can read" books and a short list for proficient, accomplished readers.

About This Book

With thousands of children's books in print today and several thousand new titles published each year how does one select 101 titles?

Even with such a vast list of titles, the majority of these books come and go rapidly with little fanfare. But there are those that stay, find a niche for themselves and pass the test of time. Those are the stories we consider classics or near classics. There are also those that we think might well become classics. So many of the stories in their sturdy library bindings are still on school library shelves. Many have been published in paperback form and are found in class-room collections. Most are still in print. Those are the titles teachers and librarians read to and use with students.

Using many different resources, I gathered together 101 titles recommended for children in the last 30-plus years of my school and public library experience. They are full-bodied stories, that have a beginning, middle and end—stories that leave the reader with a satisfied feeling of "oh, that was a good story."

Suggestions for Using this Book

- Because the clues follow the sequence of the story, the teacher/librarian and the reader can discuss, "and what happened next?"

- The clues in the puzzle can be used as discussion questions for the student and teacher/librarian.

- The students can complete the puzzle independently.

- Students can complete the puzzle with teacher/librarian.

- To use in a group, make a transparency. Have students in turn fill in the puzzle.

- Use as an introduction to an author, encouraging students to read more books in the series or other titles by that author.

- Read the book to a student or group of students, then have the students complete the puzzle independently or as a group.

Abigail Takes the Wheel
Avi

1. Abigail and Tom's home was the freight boat ____.

2. They traveled from Old Port to ____ ____ ____ daily.

3. The boat delivered vegetables and it delivered Abigail and Tom to ____.

4. In the narrows one morning, two sailing ships ____.

5. Captain Bates offered to ____ the disabled ship.

6. By law, Captain Bates had to handle her ____.

7. Abigail had to ____ *Neptune* to the disabled ship.

8. Mr. Oliver, the ____ ____, became very sick.

9. Abigail and Tom had to take ____ of the freight boat.

10. *Neptune* swept by Battery Park and up the __ River.

11. A huge ship, the ____, would not let them pass.

12. Abigail shouted, "____ engines" to avert a disaster.

13. At pier ____-____, they ran into another disaster.

14. They averted that disaster by continuous ____ blowing.

15. Abigail had to keep both ships from ____ the pier.

16. She succeeded, but was very, very ____.

17. After school, the ____ of both ships waited for Abigail and Tom.

18. The crew ____ Captain Abigail and First Mate Tom.

The Adventures of Captain Underpants
Dav Pilkey

1. George and Harold were the kings of ____ jokes.

2. Through their comics they created hundreds of ____.

3. But their ____ hero of all was Captain Underpants.

4. George and Harold caused great trouble in _____.

5. Mr. Krupp, the principal, ____ everything about the boys.

6. One day, he caught them red-handed with a ____ tape.

7. He ____ the boys to do whatever he wanted.

8. But George and Harold got tired of ____ to Mr. Krupp's whims.

9. They ordered a 3-D ____ through the mail.

10. George and Harold put Mr. Krupp under their ____.

11. Now Mr. Krupp ____ their every command.

12. They discovered he was a ____ admirer of Captain Underpants.

13. They made him the ____ Captain Underpants.

14. After foiling a bank robbery they encountered ____.

15. They led the robots to the ____ Dr. Diaper.

16. They defeated Dr. Diaper with the help of ___ doggy doo-doo.

17. The boys ____ succeeded in de-hypnotizing Mr. Krupps.

18. But the sound of ____ fingers caused a problem.

Agapanthus Hum and the Eyeglasses
Joy Cowley

1. The moment Agapanthus woke up a ___ started inside her.

2. Agapanthus's parents were worried about her ___.

3. One day her glasses slipped off and she _____ on them.

4. Her parents assured her they could ___ the glasses.

5. Agapanthus's parents always _____ her activities.

6. Agapanthus put a _____ _____ over her head to protect her glasses.

7. Mother suggested Agapanthus put her glasses in Mother's _____.

8. Agapanthus's parents took her to the _____ show.

9. Good little Mommy wore Agapanthus's _____ necklace to the show.

10. Disaster struck when Daddy bought Aganpanthus _____ ice cream.

11. Agapanthus fantasized she was a _____ acrobat.

12. After the show, Agapanthus's parents needed to _____ her up.

13. But they could not find any ___.

14. Finally her parents found a lady with ___ glasses.

15. Agapanthus realized the lady was the _____ of the show.

16. The lady _____ the sticky ice cream off Agapanthus.

17. The lady gave her glasses to her own _____ when she performed.

18. That is what the ___ acrobats do.

Amber Brown Is Not a Crayon
Paula Danziger

1. Amber and Justin have done everything together since ____.

2. Their class is going to study and do projects about ____.

3. Amber gets so tired of everyone ____ her about her name.

4. At lunch, Justin was miserable about the message in his ____ cookie.

5. Justin's father accepted a new job in ____.

6. When Justin's family ____ their house, Justin will leave New Jersey.

7. Months went by but one day Amber's worst nightmare came ____.

8. Justin and his family went on an ____ trip to buy a house in Alabama.

9. Amber has five ____ to accept the fact that Justin is leaving.

10. Amber can't accept that Justin threw away their ____ ____ ball.

11. Amber worried about how she would ever find a new best ____.

12. Mom tried to help Amber by sharing ____ double fudge brownies.

13. Amber got so mad at Justin that she stopped ____ to him.

14. Amber knows anger doesn't help. She wonders how she'll ever get along ____ Justin.

15. Today their class has a ____ ____ party for Justin.

16. Justin and Amber make up and she finally accepts that he is ____.

17. Maybe some day Justin and Amber will ____ again.

18. Whenever Amber thinks of ____ grade, she will think of Justin.

Amelia Bedelia
Peggy Parish

1. Amelia Bedelia was to follow the list of ____.

2. But first, Amelia Bedelia decided to bake a ____ meringue pie.

3. The first item on the list was to ____ the towels.

4. Next, Amelia Bedelia was to ____ the furniture.

5. The third item on the list was to draw the ____.

6. Then Amelia Bedelia was to put out the ____.

7. Imagine anyone wanting to ____ the rice.

8. Amelia Bedelia wondered why anyone would trim a ____.

9. Amelia Bedelia also wondered if she should ____ the chicken as a he or she.

10. Mrs. Rogers was angry and ready to ____ Amelia Bedelia.

11. But Mr. Rogers just ____ Amelia Bedelia's pie.

12. Amelia Bedelia ____ to understand Mrs. Rogers's directions.

Amos and Boris
William Steig

1. Amos was a ____ who loved the ocean.

2. He wanted to ____ to the other side of the ocean.

3. He built a boat, named it the ____ and set off.

4. Amos ____ being on board his ship on the ocean.

5. But one night he ____ right off the ship and was lost at sea.

6. The next day, a ____ named Boris rescued Amos.

7. Amos and Boris became very close ____.

8. Boris took Amos home before going off to ____.

9. Years later, a ____ washed Boris up on Amos's beach.

10. The two friends ____ each other.

11. Amos got two ____ to push Boris back into the ocean.

12. The two friends knew they would never ____ each other.

Annabel the Actress Starring in Just a Little Extra
Ellen Conford

1. Annabel is sure her big ____ is about to happen.

2. The Silver Tree Company has come to Westfield to make a ____.

3. Annabel's absolute favorite ____, her idol, will be the star.

4. And the Silver Tree Company will actually be using ____ in the movie.

5. Everybody in Westfield wants to be in the ___ scene.

6. Annabel stages a big show to get ____.

7. It works! She actually gets to meet ____ McCall.

8. The director gives Annabel a ___ so he can get on with the show.

9. She has to cross the street, look up at the sky and ____.

10. Two hours later, Annabel is still ____ to go on.

11. Finally, it is her turn to ____ off her talents.

12. On the third take, her ____-____ stick and Annabel falls down.

13. She gets kicked in the ankle and someone yells, "____. ____ ____!"

14. Annabel cannot ____ it is all over.

15. She has to wait ____ long months to see herself act.

16. She is the only one in that scene to have a ____ ____.

17. Then Annabel saw herself disappear in the ____ ____ cloud.

18. Hoping to be remembered, Annabel writes a ____ ____ to her idol.

Arthur's Computer Disaster
Marc Brown

1. Arthur begged and begged to use Mom's ____.

2. He really wanted to play Deep, ____ Sea.

3. He claimed it was the ____ game ever.

4. Arthur just had to find the ____, the secret to the universe.

5. The next day, Mom had to go to the ____ unexpectedly.

6. Arthur and Buster played the game against Mom's ____.

7. Arthur even had to give in to D. W.'s ____.

8. In the midst of playing, the ____ crashed to the floor.

9. The computer ____ went blank.

10. Arthur and Buster just had to ____ ____ before Mom got home.

11. Even their friend, the ____, couldn't find the problem.

12. Arthur ____ until after supper.

13. As Mom went to the computer, Arthur ____ his misdeed.

14. Mom said all that was needed was to jiggle the ____.

15. Arthur's punishment was no computer games for a ____.

16. Arthur and D. W. waited for Mom to come say ____ ____.

17. But Mom didn't come—she was ____ on finding the treasure!

18. Marc Brown has written a ____ of books about Arthur.

Babar Loses His Crown
Laurent de Brunhoff

1. The Babar family is going on a trip to ___.

2. Babar packs his ____ in a small red bag.

3. When they arrive in Paris, Babar discovers he has the ____ red bag.

4. Zaphir thinks the ____ man picked up the wrong red bag.

5. They all set out to ____ the man.

6. They do not find him in the ____ tower.

7. During a boat ride, they spy him on a ___.

8. They follow many ____ alarms in vain.

9. Then they chase him down a ____ but do not catch him.

10. They finally give up and return to the ____.

11. Babar is going to have to go to the ___ bareheaded.

12. Because he is a ____, he does not like to do this.

13. At the entrance to the opera, a man ____ into Babar.

14. Both the man and Babar have a small ____ bag.

15. The man is in the orchestra. His bag contains a ____.

16. It turns out to be a ____ night after all.

A Bargain for Frances
Russell Hoban

1. Frances is going to play with her ___ Thelma.

2. Then Mother reminds Frances of the ____ she has had with Thelma.

3. Thelma always seems to get the ____ of Frances.

4. Frances tells Thelma about the china tea set she is ____ for.

5. Thelma convinces Frances her ____ tea set is best.

6. Thelma talks Frances into ____ her tea set from her.

7. Later, Frances sees Thelma buy the ___ tea set Francis wanted.

8. Frances puts a ____ in the plastic sugar bowl.

9. Frances reminds Thelma about their no ____ policy.

10. Then Frances ____ Thelma into wanting the tea set back.

11. Thelma tries to say she left some ___ in the sugar bowl.

12. Thelma and Frances ____ the money and the tea set.

13. Thelma is not ____ about Frances besting her.

14. The two decide being friends is better than being ____.

15. They promise to ____ with each other from now on.

16. Both Frances and Thelma learned a valuable ____.

Beans Baker, Number Five
Richard Torrey

1. Beans dreamed while Coach Munhall handed out the ____.

2. He wanted so very much to wear his hero's number ____-____.

3. He could not ____ it when Coach gave that number to Sheldon.

4. Coach gave Beans ____ ____ Haskins's old number five.

5. Beans could not take the teasing, so he decided to ____.

6. Lindsay and Chester helped Beans ____ his mind.

7. But Beans still had to sit on the bench because he had missed ____.

8. However, Beans was supposed to be ____ just in case he was needed.

9. The other team was ahead ____ to nothing.

10. In the bottom of the ____, Lindsay and Chester got hits.

11. Sheldon, showing off, ____ up to the plate.

12. Suddenly, Sheldon started to shake and then he ____.

13. Coach yelled for Beans to come ____ for Sheldon.

14. The other team jeered when Beans had two ____.

15. But due to a comedy of errors Beans scored a ____ run.

16. Then Beans knew that a ____ is just a number.

Beezus and Ramona
Beverly Cleary

1. Beezus thought four-year-old Ramona was ____.

2. Ramona's main problem was her ____.

3. Ramona's ____ ears were embarrassing to Beezus, too.

4. Ramona simply delighted in being ____ far too often.

5. She thought it was fun to take one ____ out of every apple.

6. Mother asked Beezus how she wanted to celebrate her ____.

7. Beezus wanted her favorite ____ Beatrice to come to dinner.

8. Ramona invited her whole nursery school class to come to a ____.

9. But, she did not bother to tell her ____ about it.

10. Beezus saved the day by having an indoor ____.

11. Mother said it was just an ____ thing with Ramona.

12. So far, Beezus's tenth birthday had been ____.

13. But Ramona was up to her old ____.

14. She ruined the cake ____ so Mother had to start again.

15. Then Beezus ____ something bad coming from the oven.

16. Ramona had put her doll in the oven pretending she was ____.

17. Aunt Beatrice ____ the day by bringing a bakery cake.

18. Now Beezus knows that she can't love Ramona all the ____.

Betsy-Tacy
Maud Hart Lovelace

1. Betsy and Tacy became friends at Betsy's ____ birthday party.

2. The girls had a lovely private place that had been a ____ box.

3. Betsy loved kindergarten but at first Tacy was ___ and unhappy.

4. ____ loved to tell stories that always involved the two friends.

5. Betsy helped console Tacy after baby ____ died.

6. The leftover Easter egg dye was perfect for bottled colored ___.

7. Betsy and Tacy were amazed when Mrs. Benson gave them two ____ for two bottles.

8. When summer came, the girls were able to ____ all day long.

9. And they never ____ ran out of things to do.

10. The girls were fascinated by the big ____ colored house.

11. Betsy and Tacy brought great ____ to every activity.

12. Julia and Betsy came home from a visit to find a baby ____.

13. Betsy was sad because she was no longer the baby of the ____.

14. This time, however, Betsy was ____ by Tacy.

15. A family moved into the big house at the end of the ____.

16. A little girl named ____ made the girls a trio.

17. The girls' lives were ____ but so different from today.

18. The reader can follow the stories of the girls until Betsy ____.

Big Max
Kin Platt

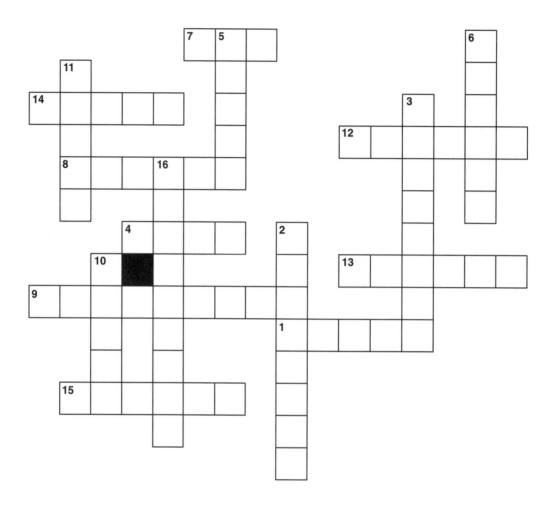

1. The King of Pooka _____ called Big Max, the world's greatest detective.

2. His prize _____, Jumbo, had been stolen.

3. Big Max always traveled by _____.

4. The king showed Big Max rooms of _____ and jewels.

5. Big Max searched everywhere for _____.

6. He announced that Jumbo had not been _____.

7. Big Max sat down to rest on a cake of _____.

8. Max found _____ and tears outside the high wall.

9. The trail led the two of them to a _____.

10. Then they heard a very loud _____.

11. They continued until they came upon a birthday _____.

12. Jumbo was celebrating his birthday with his _____.

13. The king asked Big Max how he _____ the case.

14. Big Max told him about the _____ of ice.

15. And how he realized that the evidence had _____.

16. They all enjoyed Jumbo's _____ birthday cake.

The Boxcar Children
Gertrude Chandler Warner

1. The ____ children stood in front of the baker's window.

2. They had no parents and felt their ____ did not want them.

3. They offered to work in return for a place to ____.

4. They quickly ____ ____ when they overheard the baker's conversation.

5. They found an abandoned ____ and decided to make it their home.

6. They adopted a dog who came to them with a ____ in its paw.

7. They found most of the things they needed in the ____.

8. For money, Henry went into town and worked ____ ____ for Dr. Moore.

9. On Saturday, the children worked together to build a ____ pool.

10. Henry volunteered the others to pick ____ for Dr. Moore.

11. Dr. Moore read an interesting item in the ____.

12. The children's only relative was a very ____ man.

13. James Henry Alden sponsored a ____ day every year.

14. Dr. Moore enticed Henry to enter the ____ ____ ____ race.

15. Later, the younger girl, ____, became very ill.

16. Dr. Moore took her and the others to his ____.

17. Henry ____ out they were related to James Henry Alden.

18. The children and their boxcar went to live in a ____ home.

Breakout at the Bug Lab
Ruth Horowitz

1. Our ____ worked with all kinds of bugs in a lab.

2. Our favorite bug was Max the giant ____.

3. The lab was to be renamed the Ruby L. Gold ____ Center.

4. We were invited to the ____ in honor of the change.

5. When we arrived, Leo and I fed Max his ____ food.

6. When it was time to go, somehow Max was ____.

7. Finally we found him hanging by his feet from the ____.

8. If people saw him loose, they would ____.

9. A ____ tried to help us get him down but nothing worked.

10. She asked us to get her some ____ bands.

11. She told us she was called ____ Lil when she was young.

12. She hit Max with one ____ and down he came.

13. We got Max back into his ____ just in time.

14. At the ____-cutting ceremony we found out who the lady was.

15. That night, we were all on the TV ____ program.

16. We never ____ Mom what happened.

Buford the Little Bighorn
Bill Peet

1. Buford's ____ had grown out of control.

2. He could not climb the mountains with his ____.

3. He had to go down to the ____ where it was flat.

4. He joined a herd of cattle to use as a ____.

5. But Buford was in trouble when ____ season began.

6. Hunters spotted him from a ____.

7. Buford tried to escape to the ____.

8. He left a ____ behind him in the snow.

9. Buford lost his balance, flipped and his horns became ____.

10. The hunters went sprawling into the ____.

11. Buford ended up at a ski ____.

12. Today, Buford is their ____ attraction.

Cam Jansen and the Mystery of the Dinosaur Bones
David Adler

1. Jennifer Jansen was known for her ____ memory.

2. Everybody called her "____ ____," then shortened it to Cam.

3. When Cam wanted to recall her memory, she said ____.

4. Cam and Eric were on a class trip to the ____.

5. The guide, Janet Tyler, took the class into the ____ room.

6. Cam discovered that ____ of the Coelophysis bones were missing.

7. Janet Tyler argued with Cam and ____ ____ believe her.

8. Later, Cam compared her mind's eye with Eric's ____.

9. They biked back to the museum but were caught by a ____.

10. Cam saw a truck advertising the wrong ____ of milk.

11. The milkman had stolen the bones for the ____.

12. She planned to bury the bones then ____ them for credit.

13. Cam and Eric foiled the thieves by blowing ____.

14. They ____ and called the museum director.

15. The museum recovered the bones and ____ the guide.

16. This Cam Jansen is the first in a series of ____ books.

The Camel Who Took a Walk
Jack Tworkov

1. It was that special time in the forest, ____ night and day.

2. The tiger was lying ____ at the foot of a tree.

3. A ____ camel was taking her morning stroll.

4. The tiger planned to attack when the camel reached the ____ of the tree.

5. The monkey decided to drop a ____ on the tiger's head.

6. The camel was completely ____ of all of this.

7. A little squirrel planned to ____ the monkey's tail.

8. A small ____ planned to jump on the squirrel's head.

9. The camel had almost ____ the shadow of the tree.

10. Everyone was getting ____ to act.

11. The camel let out an awful ____.

12. She turned around and ____ happened.

Caps for Sale
Esphyr Slobodkina

1. Once there was a ____ who sold caps.

2. He carried his caps on his ____ over his own cap.

3. He called out everywhere, "____ cents a cap."

4. One day, he could not ____ any caps.

5. No sales, no money so he took a ____ in the country.

6. Resting under a tree, he went to ____.

7. When he woke up, all his caps were ____.

8. Up in a tree, every ____ wore a cap.

9. He could not get them to ____ his caps.

10. He threw his own cap on the ____ and walked away.

11. Then all the caps came ___ down from the tree.

12. He put the caps back on top of his own ____ cap.

13. He walked back to ____ to try again to sell his caps.

14. Do you think he had great ____?

The Captain Contest
Matt Christopher

1. Dewey and Bundy signed up for the _____ soccer league.

2. Dewey had a _____ about entering the team logo contest.

3. The team _____ only Bundy would enter the contest.

4. Bundy was a natural _____ but had no art talent.

5. Bundy imagined a _____ pouncing on a soccer ball.

6. Entries for the contest were due the day of the _____ game.

7. In the event of one entry, that _____ would win.

8. Dewey knew his logo was really _____ than Bundy's.

9. But he couldn't possibly _____ against his best friend.

10. After agonizing, Dewey told Bundy of his _____.

11. As of that moment, Bundy was no longer his _____.

12. Suddenly, Bundy had a momentous _____.

13. He got the _____ to do something very unusual.

14. The _____ called the team together after the first win.

15. He told them there was only _____ entry for the contest.

16. He announced that _____ had won the contest.

17. But Dewey gave the credit to _____ as it was his idea.

18. This title is the first in the series of _____ Cats.

The Case of the Puzzling Possum
Cynthia Rylant

1. Bunny Brown is considered the ____ of the team of two.

2. Jack Jones is considered the ____ of the team of two.

3. At each visit, Jack comments on Bunny's ____ collection.

4. Their new case concerns the theft and return of a ____.

5. Jack and Bunny check the music store for ____ to the case.

6. Bunny finds a piece of straw and ____ foot prints.

7. That leads her to the sign about a ___.

8. They decide to attend but without ____ ____, the store's owner.

9. At the farm, there were ____ taxis lined up.

10. Bunny and Jack had suspicions about a young ____.

11. They decide to ____ him after the event.

12. Until then, they decide to have ____ at the event.

13. The suspicious character leads them to the ____ store.

14. They nab the thief in the act and he pleads ____.

15. They work out a ____ for the thief to be able to pay.

16. Then they go home and Jack ____ up the spilled food.

Charlotte's Web
E. B. White

1. Fern saved Wilbur's life as he was the _____ of the litter.

2. When Wilbur was six weeks old, Fern had to sell him to Uncle _____.

3. Wilbur was lonely and needed love and a _____.

4. A strange _____ came to Wilbur in the darkness.

5. In the morning, he discovered Charlotte, a _____.

6. Summer came and Fern visited the farm and Wilbur almost _____.

7. Templeton, the _____, was known for storing everything in his home.

8. Wilbur discovered soon he would be turned into _____ bacon and ham.

9. Charlotte promised Wilbur that somehow she would _____ him.

10. Fern's mother was _____ about Fern's talk about the animals.

11. Wilbur was saved once by the _____ odor of Templeton's egg.

12. Charlotte began to weave _____ to keep her promise.

13. Mr. Zuckerman tried to explain the _____ on his farm.

14. Every night, Charlotte wove a new _____ in her web.

15. Dr. Dorian told Fern's _____ not to worry about her.

16. Summer was over and Charlotte had little _____ left.

17. Wilbur will have a long _____ thanks to Charlotte.

18. Charlotte died but she accomplished her _____ _____.

The Chocolate Touch
Patrick Skene Catling

1. John's one big problem was being a pig about ___.

2. John would never share any candy, especially ___.

3. One day, John's parents noticed spots on John's ___.

4. John couldn't understand how eating candy could ____ his mother.

5. John found an ____ coin lying right on the sidewalk.

6. He ____ it on a box of chocolates at an unfamiliar candy shop.

7. Beneath all the wrappings, was one tiny ____ ball of chocolate.

8. The next morning, everything he ate ____ like chocolate.

9. At school, everything he touched ____ into chocolate.

10. At rehearsal, even John's ____ turned into chocolate.

11. At Susan's party, the ____ turned to chocolate.

12. He found the candy store was now only an ____ lot.

13. Even Dr. Cranium's ____ turned to chocolate.

14. His mother cried when told John had Dr. Cranium's ____.

15. When John ____ her, she turned into chocolate.

16. John rushed away and found the candy store had ____.

17. Everything John had touched was now in the ____.

18. John confessed his guilt and all changed back to ___.

Click, Clack, Moo: Cows That Type
Doreen Cronin

1. Farmer Brown had a most unusual ____.

2. The cows had somehow ____ an old typewriter in the barn.

3. It was bad enough that they ____ all day.

4. Now they were beginning to ____ with him.

5. The first typed note asked for ____ blankets.

6. When Farmer Brown refused the request, they went on ____.

7. The latest note said "____, no milk today."

8. If that wasn't enough, now the ____ had the same demand.

9. The next sign said "____, no milk, no eggs."

10. Farmer Brown ____ they produce milk and eggs.

11. ____ was the messenger as he was a neutral party.

12. The other animals tried in vain to ____ on the meeting.

13. The next morning, Farmer Brown received an ____.

14. The cows offered to ____ the typewriter for blankets.

15. Farmer Brown ____ and brought the blankets.

16. But the next morning, a new note requested a ____ ____.

Clifford the Big Red Dog
Norman Bridwell

1. Emily _____ has a dog named Clifford.

2. Clifford is the biggest, _____ dog on the street.

3. Emily Elizabeth loves to _____ way up high on Clifford's back.

4. She and Clifford have great fun playing _____ together.

5. Sometimes Clifford makes _____.

6. Clifford does have some bad _____.

7. At the zoo, Clifford runs after _____.

8. Emily admits Clifford does eat and ___ a lot.

9. However, he is a really great _____.

10. And the bad guys don't _____ her anymore.

11. Clifford didn't win a _____ at the dog show.

12. But Emily wouldn't _____ Clifford for any other dog.

Cloudy with a Chance of Meatballs
Judi Barrett

1. One night, ____ told us the best tall tale bedtime story.

2. The adventure happened in the town of Chewand-____.

3. Everyone's food came from the ____.

4. The ____ came three times a day.

5. Sometimes there would be storms of ____.

6. Another day the town was tied up by ____.

7. After a while the size of the food became ____.

8. The sanitation department could not ____ the leftovers.

9. In order to survive, the people had to ____ Chewandswallow.

10. They made rafts of stale ____ and sailed away.

11. They had to adjust to getting their food at a ____.

12. The next day, we imagined we saw ___ atop our snow hill.

Corduroy
Don Freeman

1. Corduroy was the name of a small brown ___.

2. Corduroy lived in the ____ department of a big store.

3. He wanted so very much for someone to ____ him.

4. One day, a little girl _____ to buy him.

5. But her mother said he had lost a ____.

6. That night, Corduroy decided to fix his ____ overalls.

7. Corduroy accidentally stumbled on the ____.

8. In the mattress department he caused a big ____.

9. The noise brought the ____ watchman running.

10. The night watchman returned Corduroy to the ____ where he belonged.

11. In the morning, the little girl, ____, returned.

12. She had enough money in her ____ ____ to buy Corduroy.

13. Lisa made Corduroy his own little ____ in her room.

14. Lisa ____ Corduroy's strap with a thread and needle.

15. Now Corduroy had the ____ he always wanted.

16. But best of all, Corduroy had a ____.

Curious George
H. A. Rey

1. George was a very curious little ____.

2. George lived in the continent of ____.

3. The man with the ____ ____ brought George to the city.

4. When the man left, George was very curious about the ____.

5. By mistake, George dialed the ____ ____.

6. The angry firemen captured George and put him in ____.

7. George ____ when the watchman hit his head.

8. George wanted a bright ____ balloon.

9. The bunch of balloons broke free and George ____ away.

10. George landed on the top of a ____ light.

11. The man came along in his car and ____ George.

12. The man took George to a new home in the ____.

Dance with Rosie
Patricia Reilly Giff

1. Rosie could not wait to sign up for ____ lessons with Miss Deirdre.

2. Her dream was to become a ballerina like her ____, Genevieve.

3. Tommy Murphy and Rosie were no longer best ___.

4. Rosie and her friend Karen took the lessons ____.

5. Karen and Rosie had the wrong ____. The class was full.

6. Rosie was eager to feel the ____ of happiness her teacher talked about.

7. Karen and Rosie tried to take the lessons by watching through the ____.

8. Then they ____ into the studio to practice and got caught.

9. Rosie and Karen were allowed to join the ___.

10. Everything was a complete ____ at the first lesson.

11. In the meantime, Tommy and Rosie were still ____.

12. The problem had something to do with the ____ nest.

13. Grandpa shared a picture of ____ who became Genevieve.

14. He explained how it takes years to be a real ____.

15. He said we must use our ____ to figure things out.

16. Rosie realized Tommy thought Karen had taken his ____.

17. Rosie was happy because she ____ with her best friend.

18. Today Rosie is plain Rosie but someday she will be ____.

Danny and the Dinosaur Go to Camp
Syd Hoff

1. Danny takes his friend the dinosaur to ____ with him.

2. The dinosaur is really pleased to have a ____.

3. However, the dinosaur ____ every game the kids play.

4. At lunch, the dinosaur finishes all the ____.

5. When they write letters home, the dinosaur asks for ____.

6. When the kids are tired of ____ they ride on the dinosaur's back.

7. The dinosaur has plenty of ____ for marshmallows.

8. At bedtime, the ____ is too small for the dinosaur.

9. The dinosaur takes his ____ and sleeps outside on the ground.

10. Be sure to read the ____ book about Danny and the dinosaur.

Dinosaurs Before Dark
Mary Pope Osborne

1. Jack and Annie had never seen the tree house ____.

2. The tree house was completely filled with ____.

3. Suddenly, a flying ____ flew straight at them.

4. The tree house began ____ crazily.

5. When it stopped, it was not in the same ____ tree.

6. Annie made friends with the reptile and named him ____.

7. As they started exploring, Jack found a ____ medallion.

8. Annie found a valley full of nests of tiny ____.

9. Suddenly, they saw a ____ rex racing towards them.

10. They dashed up the ladder but Jack returned for his ____.

11. The giant dinosaur was ____ Jack and the tree house.

12. The friendly reptile landed and Jack ____ on his back.

13. After a lovely flight, Jack hurried up the ____ ladder.

14. To get home, Jack and Annie made a ____ on a book.

15. Back home, they discovered ____ had stood still.

16. Jack had proof that the tree house was ____.

17. Jack and Annie knew they would be back ____.

18. *Dinosaurs Before Dark* is the ____ book in this series.

Don't Fidget a Feather!
Erica Silverman

1. Duck and Gander are ____ with each other.

2. They both claim to be the ____.

3. They decide to have a ____ in place contest.

4. Neither moved when a ____ buzzed them.

5. Neither moved when a horde of ____ played on them.

6. Neither moved as a cluster of ____ swarmed them.

7. The ____ blew and knocked them about.

8. Neither moved when a ____ captured them.

9. They watched the fox prepare a big pot of ____.

10. Gander was ____ to be cooked.

11. But ____ broke the freeze and scared the fox away.

12. The two friends ate the fox's ____ stew.

Elmer
David McKee

1. The whole herd of ____ was almost the same color.

2. Except for Elmer who was a ____.

3. It was Elmer who kept the whole herd ____.

4. But Elmer didn't like his colors. One morning, he ____ away.

5. He found a bush covered with ____.

6. He rolled and rubbed until he was ____ all over.

7. At first the others did not ____ Elmer.

8. Then Elmer shouted, "____."

9. The ____ restored Elmer back to normal.

10. The herd decided to ____ every year.

11. On Elmer Day, the herd ____ themselves just like Elmer.

12. On that day Elmer becomes the color of an ____ elephant.

Emma's Magic Winter
Jean Little

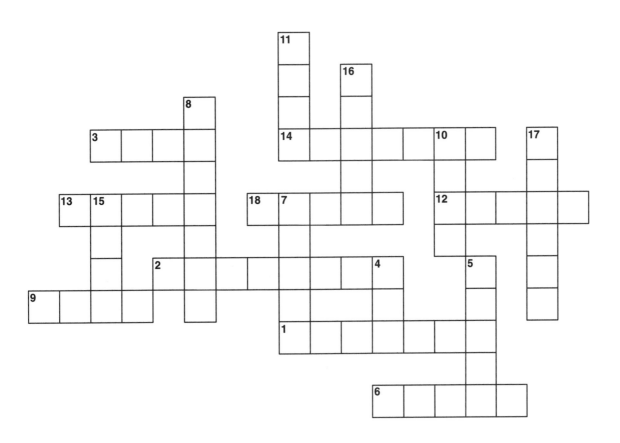

1. Emma was very shy and had problems ____ out loud.

2. She was also shy about meeting her new ____ Sally.

3. Emma went next ____ with a blueberry pie.

4. She noticed that she and Sally both had ____ boots.

5. She asked Sally if her boots were ____.

6. The girls decided to try the boots after ____.

7. They pretended each could only see the ____.

8. Then they included Sally's little ____ in on the secret.

9. Later, Emma agreed to ____ to Josh.

10. Amazingly, reading out loud to Josh was ____.

11. Later, the girls had great fun playing in the ____.

12. Emma didn't want Sally to hear Mr. Kent say "____ up."

13. On Monday, Sally read ____ and did very well.

14. Emma hung her head and could only ____.

15. At lunch, Sally had a very good ____.

16. Emma wore her boots and read in a loud clear ____.

17. All winter, the two girls ____ together.

18. When spring came, the girls got red handled jump ____.

The Five Chinese Brothers
Claire Bishop

1. The five brothers lived with their ____.

2. The first brother could ____ the sea.

3. The second brother had an ____ neck.

4. The third brother could ____ his legs.

5. The fourth brother could not be ____.

6. The fifth brother could hold his ____.

7. A small boy begged to go ____ with the first brother.

8. The small boy promised to ____ the first brother.

9. The small boy broke that promise and ____.

10. The first brother was ____ and sentenced to die.

11. Each time a brother went home ____ took his place.

12. The judge finally declared the first brother was ____.

A Flea in the Ear
Stephen Wyllie

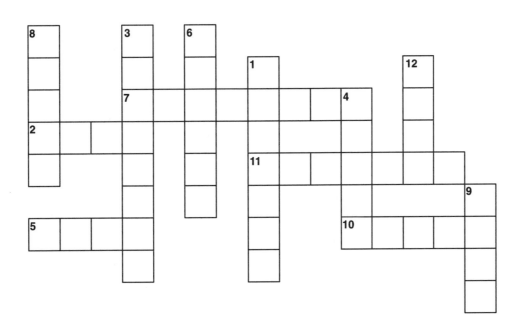

1. The ____ dog was tucking the hens into bed.

2. The ____ fox sauntered into the yard.

3. "____ ____ from my hens," ordered the dog.

4. The fox pretended he preferred juicy ____.

5. The fox noticed the dog had ____ trouble.

6. He offered a ____ remedy in exchange for some hens.

7. After scratching all night, the dog ____ the remedy.

8. He went to the pond to ____ the fleas.

9. But the fleas made a ____ with the dog.

10. While the dog was gone, the fox ____ all the hens.

11. The dog ____ the fox into going to the pond.

12. The dog saved the hens and the fleas got a new ____.

Franklin Fibs
Paulette Bourgeois

1. Franklin could do so many ____.

2. But he could not swallow ____-six flies.

3. When he told his friends he could, he ____.

4. Bear had ____ he could climb the highest tree.

5. Hawk had ____ about flying over the berry patch.

6. Beaver had ____ she could make her own dam.

7. Franklin ____ his problem to his parents.

8. They said he had quite an ____.

9. Franklin's friends ____ him to prove he could do it.

10. Franklin thought of all kinds of ____.

11. Finally he decided to try a half-____.

12. He said he could not eat them in a ____ of an eye.

13. But he baked and ate an ____ fly pie.

14. He almost claimed he could eat two pies in one ____.

15. Franklin learned his ____ the hard way.

16. The illustrations show that Franklin is a ____.

Freckle Juice
Judy Blume

1. Andrew Marcus was sure freckles would solve all his ____.

2. He was very envious of ____ freckles.

3. Sharon told Andrew she had a ____ formula to get freckles.

4. She offered to sell it to him for ____ cents.

5. The next morning, Andrew robbed his ____ ____.

6. Miss Kelly caught him ____ the formula from Sharon.

7. Miss Kelly gave it back to Andrew at ____ o'clock.

8. Andrew ____ all the ingredients together in a big blue glass.

9. He drank it and waited for something to ____.

10. The only thing Andrew got was a very upset ____.

11. Andrew then covered his face with ____ dots.

12. Everyone in the class ____ at him.

13. Miss Kelly gave him a formula for ____ freckles.

14. Andrew was surprised to learn that Nicky ____ his freckles.

15. Sharon offered Nicky another ____ formula.

16. Then she made a super-duper ____ face at Andrew.

Frederick
Leo Lionni

1. A family of ____ field mice lived in an old stone wall.

2. They all gathered food for ____ except Frederick.

3. Frederick gathered ____ ____ for the long winter days.

4. Frederick gathered ____ for winter was dreary and gray.

5. Frederick gathered ____ for winter days were very long.

6. The winter days were easy as long as ____ lasted.

7. When the food ran out, the mice were cold and ____.

8. The mice asked Frederick to ____ what he had gathered.

9. As Frederick spoke of the sun the mice felt ____.

10. As Frederick spoke of colors, the mice saw them in their ___.

11. Frederick, the word gatherer, spoke of the four ____.

12. The happy mice called Frederick a ____.

Frog and Toad Together
Arnold Lobel

1. *Frog and Toad Together* is called a ____ book.

2. Toad wrote a ____ of things to do today.

3. As each was accomplished, Toad ____ it off.

4. He was very happy until it ____ away.

5. Frog helped him remember that the final item was go to ____.

6. Frog gave Toad some ____ for a garden.

7. Nothing Toad did helped his garden to ____.

8. But Toad's garden grew when it was ____.

9. Frog and Toad could not stop eating Toad's ____.

10. Finally, they let the ___ have all that was left.

11. Frog and Toad read a book about ____.

12. They tried many stunts to pretend they were not ___.

13. Scared, they ran to Toad's house and hid ___.

14. Toad was having a very strange ____.

15. With each of his successes, Frog became ____.

16. When Frog woke him up, Toad was very ____.

17. Frog and Toad are very best ____.

George the Drummer Boy
Nathaniel Benchley

1. George was a drummer boy stationed in ____.

2. The city at the time was a colony of ____.

3. The people were unhappy at having to pay ____.

4. General Gage planned to capture a cannon at ____.

5. George's company was chosen for special ____.

6. George was told not to ask ____.

7. Later, they were rowed across the ____ River.

8. George and his friend ____ were cold and wet.

9. They saw ____ lights in the Old North Church.

10. At daybreak, they saw the ____ ____.

11. A ____ raged before George's company marched on.

12. At Concord, George's company was ____.

13. Somebody fired a shot and the soldiers returned ____.

14. George's friend was ____ in the arm.

15. At Lexington, British soldiers helped them ____.

16. This was the start of the American ____.

Gertrude, the Bulldog Detective
Eileen Christelow

1. Gertrude loved a ____ story.

2. She decided to go into the ____ business.

3. Her friends complained she was always ____.

4. One day, she received a note with instructions from the ____.

5. Gertrude was told to stake out the ____.

6. Two cats took off with a ____ in a carriage.

7. Gertrude was sure they were ____.

8. She trailed them into the ____ Movie Theater.

9. She told the ticket taker to call the ____.

10. Gertrude ____ the kidnappers to their seats.

11. The baby turned out to be a stolen ____ ____.

12. Gertrude ____ all the time Roger and Mabel wrote the note.

The Hallo-Wiener
Dav Pilkey

1. Because Oscar was ____, the other dogs teased him.

2. Today Oscar was dreaming about ____.

3. But his mother made him a giant ____ ____ bun costume.

4. Rather than hurt her ____, Oscar wore the costume.

5. The other dogs laughed and called him ____ dog.

6. At each house, there were no ____ left.

7. A huge ____ scared all the other dogs.

8. They jumped into the ____ to save themselves.

9. Oscar proved the scary thing was really two ____.

10. He saved the dogs by using his costume as a ____ ____.

11. The dogs ____ all their treats with Oscar.

12. Now the dogs call Oscar ____ sandwich.

The Hamster Chase
Anastasia Suen

1. There are ____ main characters in this story.

2. It is Amy's turn to take Mikey, the class ____, home for a week.

3. But when Amy ____, Mikey gets loose and dashes for the door.

4. The kids manage to contain him in the ____.

5. But they have to steer Mikey away from the ____.

6. They are worried that he might ____ on the wires.

7. Then Mikey runs and hides in the coat ____.

8. They hope to entice him out of his hiding place with ____.

9. They decide to make a trail of ____ seeds.

10. They begin with a line on the ____.

11. Mikey pops his ____ out to watch what they are doing.

12. They use ____ to make stairs to Mikey's cage.

13. Mikey ____ his way back into his cage.

14. Peter quickly closes the door just as Amy goes "____."

15. This all happened because Amy is allergic to Mikey's ____.

16. Read more about these kids in books by Ezra Jack ____.

Harry the Dirty Dog
Gene Zion

1. Harry was a white dog with _____ spots.

2. Harry liked everything but _____.

3. One day, he buried the brush and _____ _____.

4. Harry had fun but got very _____

5. He became a black dog with _____ spots.

6. When Harry was tired and hungry, he went _____.

7. Harry's family did not _____ him.

8. Harry finally dug up the _____ brush.

9. He carried the brush into the _____.

10. Harry _____ his family to give him a bath.

11. His family finally discovered _____ under the dirt.

12. Harry hid the brush under his _____ for another adventure.

Henry and Mudge
Cynthia Rylant

1. Henry was the only ____ in his family.

2. He didn't even have any ____ on his street.

3. His parents ____ that he could have a dog.

4. Henry had to find a very ____ dog.

5. His special dog Mudge grew out of seven ____.

6. Henry used to ____ about things as he walked to school.

7. Now he and Mudge ____ walked to school.

8. Mudge ____ everything about Henry's room.

9. And every night he went to ____ with Henry.

10. One day Mudge went for a walk ____ Henry.

11. After having fun, Mudge found he was ____.

12. Henry ____ when Mudge didn't come when he called.

13. But he knew Mudge would never ____ him.

14. So he looked and looked and ____ everywhere.

15. Finally they ____ each other.

16. Sometimes in their ____ Henry and Mudge were apart.

17. Now Henry is positive that Mudge will ____ be with him.

18. This is the first book in the Henry and Mudge ____.

Herbie Jones
Suzy Kline

1. Herbie and his friend Raymond were in the ____ reading group.

2. Herbie was the only student to receive a ____ from Miss Pinkham.

3. Herbie was surprised to receive an invitation to ____'s birthday party.

4. Herbie brought a gift of pink ____ to the birthday party.

5. A problem arose when Margie claimed the girl's bathroom was ____.

6. Herbie ____ Annabelle from the girl's bathroom.

7. Herbie wasn't sure he liked being tested by the ____ supervisor.

8. Herbie adopted two ____ living in his family's bathroom.

9. Herbie and Raymond were ___ on the class trip.

10. During lunch, they sneaked out to buy ____.

11. They got caught and Herbie got a ____ from his father.

12. Herbie's mother got a job at Dipping ____.

13. Herbie's sister ____ up his pets Gus and Spike.

14. Herbie rushed to Dipping Donuts and accused her of ___.

15. All relaxed when his mom ____ about Gus and Spike.

16. The boys and Margie ____ the reading group's name.

Hot-Air Henry
Mary Calhoun

1. Henry wanted his ____ to fly in the balloon.

2. The man said he would not fly with that ____.

3. It was the man's turn to ____.

4. At the last moment, Henry saw his chance to ____ ____.

5. His claw snagged the cord and the balloon ____away.

6. Henry and the balloon ____ across the sky.

7. Henry had a great ride but how could he get ____?

8. He finally figured out how to adjust the ____.

9. Henry met up with and chased some ____.

10. He scared an ____ away from the balloon.

11. He had to fight a goose to avoid the power lines on ____ ____.

12. Henry landed and ____ a pardon on the man's chest.

How Do Dinosaurs Say Good Night?
Jane Yolen

1. Papa comes in to say ___ and turn off the light.

2. Does a dinosaur slam his ____ and pout?

3. Does he throw his ____ bear all about?

4. Does he shout and shout to hear one more ____?

5. Does a dinosaur just open his mouth and ____?

6. Do things begin to change when ____ comes in?

7. Does a dinosaur ____his neck from side to side?

8. Does he demand a ____ ride?

9. Does a dinosaur try all sorts of ____?

10. No, he just gives a great big ____.

11. He will turn out the ____ with his tail.

12. He even ____ his tail in the bed.

13. He will show his teeth and ____ good night.

14. He will give a great big ____ and one more kiss.

How to Make an Apple Pie and See the World
Marjorie Priceman

1. If the market is closed, you may need to _____.

2. Go to _____ for a couple of armfuls of wheat.

3. For the freshest eggs from France, bring along the _____.

4. You will find the best _____ in Sri Lanka.

5. For the freshest milk, gather up an _____ cow.

6. While at sea, scoop up a jar of salty _____.

7. Cut some _____ at a plantation in Jamaica.

8. On the way home, drop off in Vermont for some _____.

9. Grind, boil, slice and mix all the _____ together.

10. After baking, invite some _____ to share the pie.

11. _____ ice cream goes so well with apple pie.

12. If the market is closed, eat the pie _____.

Hugo and the Bully Frogs
Francesca Simon

1. Hugo was a small frog with a small ____.

2. Three big mean frogs ____ on Hugo.

3. Hugo did not know how to ____ back.

4. He tried being ____ but that did not work.

5. Everyone at the pond offered ____.

6. But Hugo sighed at each suggestion and said, "____ ____."

7. Then the duck told Hugo to shout "____ ____."

8. That didn't work so the duck suggested Hugo shout "____."

9. Then, Hugo opened his mouth and ____.

10. Later, the bully frogs came back and ____ Hugo.

11. Hugo yelled and really ____ the bully frogs.

12. Now finally, Hugo is safe and ____.

The Hundred Dresses
Eleanor Estes

1. The girls enjoyed ____ on Wanda outside class.

2. They liked to play the ____ game with Wanda.

3. One reason was that Wanda was ____ from the other girls.

4. Also, Wanda lived on ____ Heights, the wrong part of town.

5. But it was days before they ____ she was absent from class.

6. Wanda said she had one ____ dresses in her closet.

7. However, Maddie worried she might become the next ____.

8. The class held two contests. The contest for girls was ____ dresses.

9. The contest for boys was designing ____.

10. The ____ of the girls' contest was Wanda.

11. All of Wanda's drawings were ____ on the classroom wall.

12. A note from Wanda's father said the family was ____.

13. Peggy and Maddie went to her ____ but Wanda was gone.

14. They wrote a ____ to Wanda about the contest.

15. A letter came from Wanda to ____ away her drawings.

16. Peggy and Maddie discovered Wanda had ____ them as models.

Ira Sleeps Over
Bernard Waber

1. Ira was invited to _____ at Reggie's house.

2. Ira was very happy but he had a _____.

3. His sister asked if he would take his _____ _____.

4. Ira said that was _____, of course not.

5. But, Ira wondered if he would be able to sleep _____ him.

6. Ira _____ all day long about what to do.

7. Ira's mom and dad said Reggie would not _____ at him.

8. His sister did not _____. She said he would.

9. Ira tried without success to get Reggie's _____.

10. Ira finally _____ and went next door to Reggie's house.

11. Reggie and Ira played lots of stuff in his _____.

12. When they were in bed, Reggie began a long _____ story.

13. Ira thinks Reggie _____ himself.

14. Reggie got up and sneaked something out of his _____.

15. It was his own teddy bear named _____ _____.

16. Ira went _____ and got his own teddy bear.

17. When he got back, Reggie was _____ asleep.

18. So _____ _____ and Ira went to sleep too.

The Island of the Skog
Steven Kellogg

1. The mice had a party on National _____ Day.

2. The party was interrupted by the _____.

3. The mice decided to sail away and find a peaceful _____.

4. _____ declared he would be the captain.

5. First they mistakenly sailed towards the _____ Pole.

6. They found an island occupied by a being called a _____.

7. The mice think this being is a huge ___.

8. They fired twelve ___ and took over the island.

9. They made a plan to _____ the being.

10. The plan worked but the being came _____ apart.

11. The being was actually a very lonely little _____.

12. They decided to build a _____ and live together.

Jack and the Beanstalk
Richard Walker

1. Jack was not lazy whenever he sniffed an ____.

2. Jack had to sell ____ because he and his mom had no food.

3. Jack exchanged the cow for six ____ beans.

4. Jack's mom threw the beans out the ____.

5. During the night, an ____ beanstalk grew and grew.

6. Jack climbed up and up to a huge ____.

7. An old woman ____ to give Jack some food.

8. She warned him to ____ when the giant came.

9. ____ ____ ____ ____ alerted Jack that the giant was coming.

10. Jack watched the giant play with his ____ riches.

11. Then Jack slid down the stalk for some ____.

12. Back at the top, Jack ____ the sack and the goose.

13. All was well until the ___ gave him away.

14. The giant woke up and gave ____.

15. The beanstalk swayed and bent but did not ____.

16. Jack grabbed and pulled the rope with all his ____.

17. The giant ____ off into space.

18. Jack and the others lived happily ____ ____.

The Joy Boys
Betsy Byars

1. J. J. and Harry were going to ride the ___.

2. The boys did not understand what Mr. Joy ____ to them.

3. While playing cowboy, J. J. saw the ____ coming after them.

4. The boys had to dash for safety ____ the fence.

5. Mrs. Joy told the boys not to get their ____ muddy.

6. The boys took off their shoes, then made a huge pile of ____ ____.

7. They used each other as a ____ target.

8. But they could not understand why Mrs. Joy sounded so ____.

9. Then they realized she thought they were ____.

10. But an argument over Bono led to a ____ fight.

11. Later the boys apologized and said they were ____.

12. The boys set up a tent to catch a ____ animal.

13. They got ____ when they heard strange noises.

14. They pulled their ____ bags over their heads.

15. J. J. peeked and saw Bono's long ____ through the flap.

16. The boys fell asleep with Bono tucked in ____ them.

Julian's Glorious Summer
Ann Cameron

1. Julian ____ ____ stories only when it is necessary.

2. Julian's best friend is ____.

3. Julian's ____ is his best friend's new bicycle.

4. He ____ and said that he has to work around the house.

5. So Julian's ____ gives him lots of chores.

6. Julian finally admits he ____ bicycles.

7. By the end of the third week, Julian is still ____.

8. Gloria and ____ are riding the bicycle together.

9. On payday, Julian's father gives him ____ and a race car book.

10. Then, he surprises Julian with a new ____.

11. Julian wants to ____ the bicycle to the store.

12. He says people ____ off bicycles.

13. Gloria says the fun is bigger than the ____.

14. Julian practices riding using ____ blocks.

15. Julian is surprised that keeping his ____ is easy.

16. Even Huey is ____ of Julian.

17. Julian and Gloria ____ to the park together.

18. Gloria looks forward to ____ with Julian.

Katy and the Big Snow
Virginia Lee Burton

1. Katy was a very big and strong red ____.

2. Katy had a bulldozer and a ____ ____.

3. The highway department said that ____ could stop Katy.

4. Katy was only used when there was a big ____.

5. One day it looked like a ____ ____ was coming.

6. It snowed until everything ____.

7. "____ ____," said Katy as she helped the police.

8. Then she plowed ___ to the Railway Station.

9. After that, she plowed out to ____ Geoppolis.

10. Katy helped the doctor get to the ____.

11. She plowed the roads for the ____ department.

12. Then she had to plow way out to the ____.

13. After helping the truck plows Katy started ____.

14. But she plowed the side roads before going home to ____.

Katy No-Pocket
Emmy Payne

1. Katy ____ had a little boy named Freddie.

2. Katy did not have a ____ to carry Freddie.

3. She asked some other ____ how they carried their babies.

4. Mrs. Crocodile carried Catherine on her ___.

5. Mrs. Monkey carried Jocko in her ____.

6. Mother birds ____ carry their babies.

7. The owl told Katy to go to the ____.

8. She saw a man with an ____ full of pockets.

9. The man tied it around Katy's ____.

10. She hippity hopped home ____ then ever before.

11. Katy became the animals' favorite ____.

12. Now Katy has more pockets than any animal in the ____.

King Emmett the Second
Mary Stolz

1. Emmett's family is moving from New York City to ____.

2. He tries without success to ____ to go.

3. One reason is his pet ____, that lives on a farm in the country.

4. When Emmett wants to go see him, he is told King Emmett is ____.

5. After apartment living, Emmett's home now is a house with two ____.

6. He slowly begins to think it might not be too ____ living here.

7. But after a couple of weeks he still misses all his ____.

8. Then his mother surprises him with his first ____.

9. He would not even try to ride it because of the ____ wheels.

10. So his father just ____ those things.

11. Emmett tries and tries to ride but he keeps ____ down.

12. The boy across the street offers to ____ him.

13. By the end of the day, ____ and Emmett are friends.

14. Now Emmett ____ everything about his new home.

15. His parents ask if he would like a pet for his ____.

16. Emmett says no, but thinks about other people's ____.

17. Emmett decides it would be nice to have a ____.

18. He will be King Emmett the Second but called ____.

The Legend of the Bluebonnet:
An Old Tale of Texas
Tomie de Paola

1. There was a great ___ in the land.

2. When the winter was over, the ____ rains did not come.

3. One small girl had a much loved ____ doll.

4. The Shaman said the Great Spirits needed a ____.

5. Each person must burn a most ____ possession.

6. No one was ____ to make a donation.

7. The small girl believed the great ____ wanted her doll.

8. That ____ she took a fire stick to the hill.

9. She built a fire and ___ her doll.

10. She ____ the ashes to the four winds.

11. The next morning the hill was covered with ____ flowers.

12. The people believed the flowers were a sign of ____.

The Legend of the Indian Paintbrush
Tomie de Paola

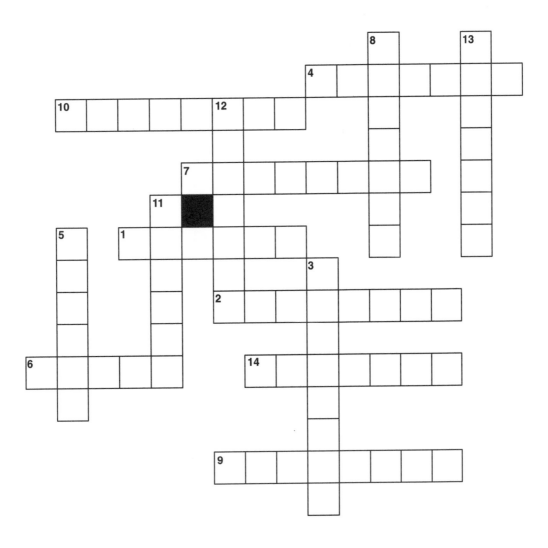

1. The boy was called Little ____.

2. Due to his size, he could not prove his ___.

3. But he could ___ stones with juices from berries.

4. The shaman believed the boy had a ____ gift.

5. When the boy was older, the dream ____ came to him.

6. His ____ of greatness would be paint and brush.

7. He would use these on a piece of pure white ____.

8. The colors would be as beautiful as the ____ sun.

9. For years, the boy painted ____ of great hunts and deeds.

10. He wanted the people to always ____ their past.

11. But he could not find the ___ of the sunset.

12. One night, he found ____ filled with paint.

13. He ____ the sunset and left the brushes behind.

14. The next day, the brushes had become beautiful ____.

The Librarian from the Black Lagoon
Mike Thaler

1. Today the class is going to visit the ____.

2. The library is way down beyond the ____ room.

3. The librarian's name is Mrs. ____.

4. The library assistant is named ____.

5. To get into the library requires several ____.

6. There, the books are ____ together.

7. The librarian reads ____ cards at story time.

8. She can also recite from the ____ decimal system.

9. The soles of the librarian's shoes stamp "____."

10. On vacation, she visits the Library of ____ every year.

11. The computer in the library uses a real ____.

12. Fortunately, the story this far is a ____.

13. The library really is a ____ place.

14. There is even a ____ mat on the floor.

15. The librarian ____ at all the children.

16. The children really ____ the library.

17. The author is really just ____ the reader.

18. This series of stories is ____.

Little Bear
Else Minarik

1. There are ____ chapters in this book about Little Bear.

2. The first chapter takes place in the ____.

3. Little Bear wants to go outside to play in the ____.

4. After several trials, Little Bear finds his ____ coat for play.

5. The second chapter is about Little Bear's ____.

6. Little Bear decides to make ____ in the pot by the fire.

7. Little Bear invites all his ____ to share with him.

8. Mother Bear surprises all with a special ____.

9. In the third chapter, Little Bear wants to fly to the ____.

10. Mother Bear says be home for ____.

11. Little Bear jumps from a tree on a ____ hill.

12. This land looks very much like Little Bear's ____.

13. Little Bear is a bear from ___, not the moon.

14. In the last chapter, Little Bear cannot ____.

15. Little Bear wants to have his ____ come true.

16. Mother Bear says only ____ wishes can come true.

17. Little Bear falls asleep after stories about ____.

18. This kind of book is a talking ____ story.

Little House in the Big Woods
Laura Ingalls Wilder

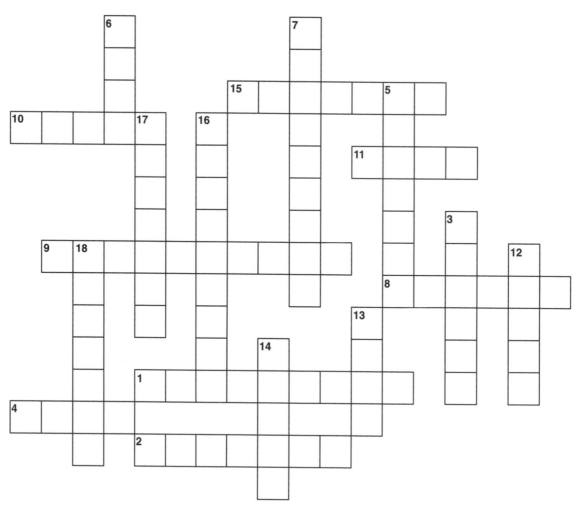

1. Laura and her family lived in a log house in the woods of ____.

2. There were no ____ stores nearby, so they were self-sufficient.

3. All fall they worked to stock food for the long ____.

4. Laura and Mary helped Ma do all the ____ inside the house and out.

5. During the long evenings, the family loved to listen to Pa's ____.

6. Laura and Mary always felt warm and ____ in the little log house.

7. The most exciting time of the year in the little log house was ____.

8. Even though they could not get to church, ____ was a special day.

9. Laura and Mary had a great time at Grandpa's ____ ____ event.

10. Spring came. The girls oiled their ____ and put them away.

11. A rare trip to ____ was a great event for the family.

12. The long summer days were filled with ____ times.

13. Laura could not help being jealous over Mary's ____.

14. When Pa found a bee tree, they had lots of ____.

15. The busiest time of the year was ____ time.

16. Especially when the ___ came to separate the wheat.

17. All was done and the family ____ in for another winter.

18. The Little House series is based on the ____ childhood.

Little Pear: The Story of a Little Chinese Boy
Eleanor Frances Lattimore

1. Little Pear lived with his family in the country of ____.

2. One side of the village was the ___ to the city.

3. On the other side of the village was a swift-flowing muddy ___ .

4. Little Pear, a ____-year-old boy, was always in some kind of trouble.

5. One day, after a squabble with some boys, he began ____ to the city.

6. Too far from home to go back, a man gave him a ride on his ___.

7. Later, the man sent Little Pear home to his village by ____.

8. Litte Pear shared candy and a ____ about a top with his friend.

9. Everyone in the village shared in the fun during the ____ ____ festival.

10. But Little Pear learned that ___ are dangerous, too.

11. Little Pear and his sister tried out their new ____.

12. The wind was so strong, Little Pear almost ____ ____ himself.

13. One day, Little Pear became ill from eating green ____.

14. Little Pear felt sorry for the canary so he gave him his ____.

15. He wanted to go to the ____ so he hid in the vegetables.

16. While waving at a boat, he ____ into the river.

17. A ____ rescued him and brought him home.

18. Little Pear ____ his family he would become a good boy.

Little Rabbit's Loose Tooth
Lucy Bate

1. Little Rabbit had her ____ loose tooth.

2. All week Little Rabbit chewed ____ foods with her loose tooth.

3. She chewed regular foods with her ___ teeth.

4. On Friday, her tooth came out into her ____ ice cream.

5. Little Rabbit said she had a ___ in her mouth.

6. She gave her tooth a ____ in cold water.

7. She ____ about what she could do with her tooth.

8. Little Rabbit decided to believe in the tooth ____.

9. She put the envelope and tooth under her ____.

10. She wondered what might happen to her ____.

11. Little Rabbit got ____ for bed.

12. She asked Mother Rabbit to ____ during the night.

13. In the morning Little Rabbit found a ____ .

14. What might happen when ____ loose tooth comes out?

Little Toot
Hardie Gramatky

1. Little Toot got his name from the sound that came out of his _____.

2. On the river where Little Toot lived, there was always work for _____.

3. But Little Toot preferred to have fun _____ river games.

4. The other tugboats called him a _____ who did not know how to work.

5. Little Toot sulked and drifted down the river with the _____.

6. He was frightened when a storm came up and he heard the _____ crashing.

7. Suddenly, up in the sky was a brilliant, flaming distress _____.

8. Little Toot saw a huge _____ liner wedged between two gigantic rocks.

9. He puffed and puffed out the signal _____.

10. In the harbor, all the boats raced to the _____.

11. But the boats could not make _____ against the sea.

12. Little Toot was scared _____ but he had to save the ship.

13. He _____ from the top of one wave to the next.

14. The great ship threw a _____ to Little Toot.

15. When a huge wave lifted the ship, he _____ it free.

16. Little Toot was blasted as a ___ all over the river.

17. Today he is one of the ___ workers on the river.

18. Try reading further _____ of Little Toot.

Little Whistle
Cynthia Rylant

1. This story takes place in a store called ____.

2. The main character is a ____ ____ named Little Whistle.

3. Little Whistle spent all day ____.

4. Every night, he put on his blue ____ ____.

5. And every night, he had a new ____.

6. Whenever Little Whistle was awake, ____ would happen.

7. Little Whistle hid his clothing in a ____ ____ during the day.

8. Whenever a toy went ____ with a child, Little Whistle was happy.

9. Little Whistle still had lots of good ____ in the store.

10. When the store was closed, everything was ____.

11. The toys did special things when the ____ were drawn.

12. Little Whistle loved to travel to ____ all the toys.

13. He loved to watch and listen to all the ____.

14. Little Whistle was happy. He did not want to be ____.

15. He wanted to ____ forever in the toy store.

16. Little Whistle was a very ____ animal.

17. Only the toys and the ____ knew about his activities.

18. Reading Little Whistle gives one a ____ fuzzy feeling.

Madeline
Ludwig Bemelmans

1. The setting of this story is ____, France.

2. ____ little girls did everything in two straight lines.

3. They ____ at the good and frowned at the bad.

4. They always left the house at half past ____.

5. Madeline was the ____ of all the little girls.

6. But she always knew how to ____ Miss Clavel.

7. One night, Madeline woke up feeling very ____.

8. The doctor pronounced it an ____.

9. Madeline was rushed to the ____.

10. Two hours later, Madeline felt much ____.

11. She proudly showed off her ___ to the other girls.

12. But that night, Miss Clavel felt something was ____.

13. All eleven girls were ____.

14. They ____ to have their appendix out too.

15. Miss Clavel told them to be grateful they were ____.

16. Read more adventures of Madeline in this ____.

Mary Moon Is Missing
Patricia Reilly Giff

1. The most popular subject in town was the Pigeon Prize ____.

2. My friend Cash and I found a ___ in a capsule dropped by a pigeon.

3. My whole ____ consisted of my brother Orlando and me.

4. He was very protective but I could read his ____ language.

5. I was thrilled when police officer Kitty and Orlando became ____.

6. However, Cash and I were determined to ____ the capsule mystery.

7. Tough Teresa provided a clue when she grabbed my ____ hard.

8. Later, Cash and I found a ____ bird in Tough Teresa's pigeon coop.

9. Kitty and I went shopping and found a gorgeous ____ dress for the party.

10. Later, I rescued who I thought was Mary Moon from the top of the ____.

11. As I wasn't positive it was her, I renamed her ____.

12. But when someone tried to ____ my pigeon, I screamed.

13. Afraid that Bird was in ____ we rowed to Muck Island.

14. All was well until the boat hit a ____.

15. We were ____ ashore and marooned on Muck Island.

16. We sent a message via Mischief to the Catfish ___.

17. But Tough Teresa came first and I ___ her in the loft.

18. But I goofed. Tough Teresa was not the ____.

19. It was my ____ that solved the mystery.

20. Police officer Kitty went off to ____ Ryan Biale.

Mike Mulligan and His Steam Shovel
Virginia Lee Burton

1. Mike Mulligan and his steam shovel ____ ____ were partners.

2. They worked as a ____ on very important projects.

3. Mike said they could dig in a day what one ____ men could in a week.

4. New types of shovels came along and put them out of ____.

5. Mike read that ___ was going to build a new town hall.

6. Mike offered to dig the cellar in one ____ or receive no pay.

7. Henry B. Swap thought he could get the cellar dug for ____.

8. Mike and his steam shovel began work at ____ ____.

9. Just as the sun went down, the cellar was ____.

10. But Mike and his steam shovel had ____ to leave a way out.

11. The steam shovel became the ____ for the new town hall.

12. And Mike became the ____ for the new town hall.

Ming Lo Moves the Mountain
Arnold Lobel

1. Ming Lo and his wife live at the _____ of a mountain.

2. The mountain brings them nothing but _____.

3. Ming Lo's wife insists that he _____ the mountain.

4. The wise man tells Ming Lo to push a _____ against the mountain.

5. Next the wise man tells Ming Lo to make a lot of _____.

6. Next the wise man tells Ming Lo to feed the _____ in the mountain.

7. The _____ from the wise man's pipe increases with each visit.

8. Finally, the wise man orders Ming Lo to perform a _____.

9. Ming Lo and his wife pack everything into _____.

10. They moved backwards with their eyes _____.

11. When they stopped, the mountain was _____ away.

12. Ming Lo and his wife _____ _____ actually move the mountain.

Miss Nelson Is Missing!
Harry Allard

1. Room 207 was the _____ behaved class in the school.

2. They would not do anything the _____ asked them to do.

3. The next day, the class had a _____.

4. Her name was Miss Viola _____.

5. The kids were sure she was a real _____.

6. She made the kids in Room 207 _____ all the time.

7. The kids felt something _____ had happened to Miss Nelson.

8. They went to the _____ to report her missing.

9. The kids in Room 207 were very _____.

10. One day Miss Nelson _____ unexpectedly.

11. Since that day, the kids have been very well _____.

12. Miss Nelson and the kids each have a _____.

Miss Rumphius
Barbara Cooney

1. ____ was a little girl who lived by the sea.

2. She grew up listening to stories of ____ places.

3. Grandfather said she must help to make the world more ____.

4. When she grew up, Miss Rumphius worked in a ____.

5. Then she traveled all over the ____.

6. She injured her back getting off a ____.

7. Miss Rumphius retired to a little house by the ____.

8. She planted a few ____ seeds.

9. The next year she discovered a huge ____ of plants.

10. Miss Rumphius wandered everywhere, ____ seeds.

11. Finally, she completed the ____ accomplishments.

12. Someday, I, too, will do what my ____ ____ did.

The Mitten
Jan Brett

1. Nicki wanted mittens knitted of ____ white as snow.

2. His grandma ____ finally agreed to knit them.

3. While Nicki was playing, one mitten ____ in the snow.

4. A tired ____ burrowed in and decided to stay.

5. Next a snowshoe ____ wiggled in, feet first.

6. They didn't argue as a hedgehog with ____ joined them.

7. An ____ swooped down and came in out of the cold.

8. The mitten really stretched when a ____ climbed in.

9. A fox poked his ____ in, then pushed all the way in.

10. They dared not fuss when a bear ____ his way in.

11. The mitten bulged and bulged but held ____.

12. A tiny meadow ____ became the last tenant.

13. When the bear ____, they exploded out of the mitten.

14. Nicki spotted his mitten on the way ____.

15. He saw his grandma watching in the ____.

16. She looked first to see if he was safe and ____.

17. Then she checked for his ____.

18. She didn't understand why one mitten was so ____.

Morris and Boris
Bernard Wiseman

1. This book consists of ____ chapters.

2. In the first chapter, Boris tries to explain ____.

3. Morris keeps coming up with different ____.

4. Boris is ____ getting frustrated.

5. Finally, Boris gives up and goes ____.

6. In chapter two, Boris tries to explain tongue ____.

7. Morris does not seem to ____.

8. Morris and Boris get into a big ____.

9. Boris gives up and goes ____.

10. A ____ asks Morris what happened.

11. In chapter three, Boris wants to play ____.

12. They are going to play hide and ____.

13. Again Morris does not play Boris's ____.

14. Morris always seems to make Boris ____

15. In this story, Boris is a ____.

16. Morris is a ____.

The Mouse and the Motorcycle
Beverly Cleary

1. Ralph and his family lived in a ____ ____ in the old inn.

2. Keith and his parents came to spend a few ____ at the old inn.

3. Ralph fell in love with Keith's ____ motorcycle.

4. Ralph secretly tried out the cycle and fell into the metal ____.

5. He was terrified when Keith ____ down and discovered him.

6. It was completely natural that they could ___ to each other.

7. The trick to making the vehicles go was to make the right ____.

8. Ralph had a glorious time ____ all around the hall.

9. He ____ Keith he would not ride the motorcycle during the day.

10. But Ralph had a bad experience with the ____.

11. To save his life, Ralph had to ____ the cycle behind.

12. Later, Keith presented Ralph with a ____ helmet.

13. Then Ralph had to ____ what happened to the motorcycle.

14. The next morning, Keith and Ralph were ____ again.

15. That night, Keith developed a high ____.

16. Ralph searched the hotel and finally found an ____.

17. He used the ____ to carry the pill to Keith.

18. The bellboy found the cycle and Keith ____ it to Ralph.

A Mouse Called Wolf
Dick King-Smith

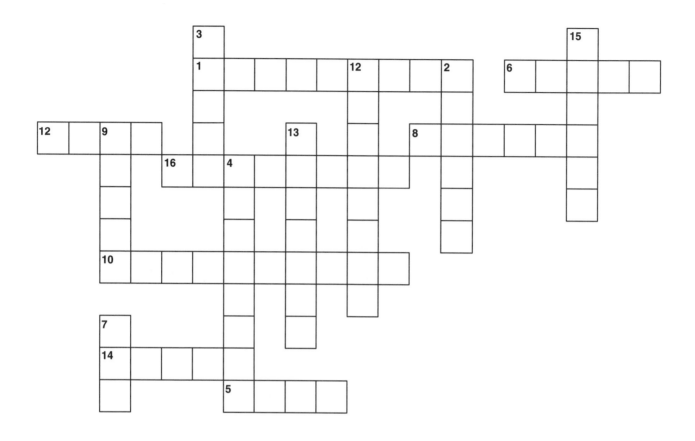

1. Because of his age and size, Wolf was given an ____ name.

2. His twelve brothers and sisters ____ him constantly.

3. Mrs. Honeybee played the ____ twice each day.

4. Wolf began to love to listen to the ____.

5. He wished so very much that he could ____.

6. He tried and discovered he had a beautiful singing ____.

7. Wolf and Mary had a scary encounter with the ____.

8. Mrs. Honeybee was shocked to hear Wolf singing an old ____.

9. Mrs. Honeybee knew Wolf could only learn the ____.

10. Mrs. Honeybee lured Wolf out of his hole with ____.

11. She earned Wolf's trust and they performed ____ daily.

12. One morning, Wolf waited and waited but she did not ____.

13. Wolf gathered up his ____and went to look for her.

14. He discovered she had fallen and hurt her ____.

15. Wolf alerted the policeman by singing at the open ____.

16. Later, Wolf ____ a special sonata for Mrs. Honeybee.

Muggie Maggie
Beverly Cleary

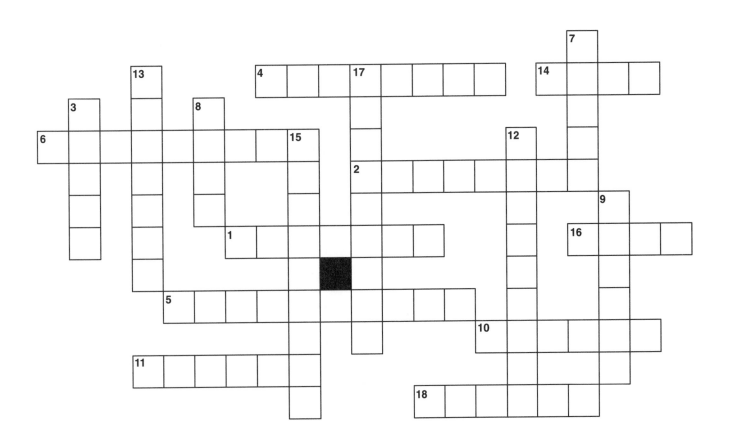

1. Maggie decided she was not going to learn cursive
   ____.

2. Maggie's parents considered her ____.

3. Maggie practiced ____ and lines that went up and
   down.

4. She decided she would rather use the ____ for writing.

5. Mrs. Leeper called Maggie's mother in for a ____.

6. The principal declared that Maggie was not ____.

7. The school psychologist said Maggie would do it
   when she was ____.

8. Maggie felt she could not ____ down now.

9. Everybody in school ____ about Maggie's decision.

10. Just to prove she could, Maggie ___ her name.

11. But she wrote ____ instead of Maggie.

12. Daddy's secretary sent her a ____ pen.

13. Maggie ____ a thank you to Mrs. Madden.

14. In school, Maggie discovered she could not ____
    cursive.

15. For several days Maggie ___ notes around the
    school.

16. She noticed her ____ on all the notes.

17. She ____ reading and writing cursive all weekend.

18. She discovered she could do it because she ____ to.

My Father's Dragon
Ruth Stiles Gannett

1. *My Father's Dragon* is the first in a series of ____ books.

2. My father, Elmer Elevator, made friends with a stray alley ___.

3. He told my father of a dragon forced to be a ____ service.

4. The story prompted Elmer to decide to ____ the baby dragon.

5. He became a ____ on a ship sailing to Cranberry.

6. In the dark of night, Elmer crossed the ____ to Wild Island.

7. Elmer soon realized the animals knew someone had ____ the island.

8. He almost got caught by the litter of his tangerine ____.

9. He found the river but ____ he was being followed.

10. Elmer escaped from the tigers through the use of ___ gum.

11. His toothbrush and ____ got him away from the rhinoceros.

12. He escaped from the ____ by using items in his knapsack.

13. The ____ were still trying to figure out the situation.

14. Elmer's next problem was with a large and fierce ____.

15. He used his ____ glasses to escape.

16. He managed to cross the river using ____ and crocodiles.

17. The baby dragon urged Elmer to ____ to rescue him.

18. Elmer worked to cut the heavy rope with his ____.

19. Finally, he succeeded and the baby dragon said, "____ ____."

20. Elmer and the dragon flew away vowing never to ___.

Nate the Great
Marjorie Weinman Sharmat

1. Nate the Great is a detective who works ____.

2. This case concerned Annie's lost ____.

3. Nate the Great wears a ____ Holmes hat.

4. Annie's drawings were all done in ____.

5. Only the drawing of Annie's ____ Fang was missing.

6. Fang ____ most everything but not the missing item.

7. Nate checked out Annie's ____ Rosamond.

8. He determined that she was ____.

9. Next, Nate checked out Annie's ____ Harry.

10. He became ____ of one of the drawings on Harry's wall.

11. The drawing was a different ____ than the rest.

12. It was ____. All the rest were red.

13. Nate announced he had ____ the case.

14. Harry had changed the drawing of Fang into a ____.

15. Nate the Great likes happy ____.

16. Nate the Great solves many cases in this ____ of books.

Owen Foote, Second Grade Strongman
Stephanie Greene

1. Owen was not happy being called ____ for his age.

2. He was embarrassed when Mrs. Jackson, the school nurse, called him a ____.

3. He wanted to be a ____ like his grandfather.

4. He wrote to his ____ for more information about his grandfather.

5. Owen was surprised that his friend Joseph was unhappy about his ____.

6. Joseph got nervous as Owen was always ____ late for school.

7. Ben, the school ____, was always trying to get the best of Owen.

8. During height and weight class, Owen got sent to the ____ office.

9. But he was complimented by a ____ grader which was cool.

10. His parents were furious at Owen's lack of good ____.

11. However, he had to pass the nurse's ____ all the time.

12. But on Monday, Mrs. Jackson was very ____ to him.

13. She said her son told her she needed a ____ aid.

14. She actually smiled at Owen and called him a late ____.

15. Finally, Owen received an ____ to his letter.

16. Eagerly he read the letter, hoping to discover the ____.

17. She wrote his grandfather's strength was in his ____.

18. Owen realized the power of ____ was within himself.

Owls in the Family
Farley Mowat

1. It all began one spring morning in Saskatoon, Saskatchewan, ____.

2. My friend Bruce and I were looking for an ____ ____.

3. Of course, I already had dozens of ____.

4. With help, we found one, but how could we get the ____ birds?

5. After a chinook, we found one bird under a pile of ____.

6. After some roast beef and bread, Wol became our ____ for life.

7. Dad helped me make a special ____ for Wol.

8. I traded my ____ knife for a companion, Weeps, for Wol.

9. It was a very long time before Wol figured out how to ____.

10. After that, I didn't worry too much about Wol's ____.

11. In fact, animals ____ the street to avoid Wol.

12. We lost first prize in the parade due to Bruce's ____.

13. Wol loved to practice all kinds of practical ____.

14. But the worst was bringing home a dead ____.

15. Wol saved us from bullies by his owl hunting ____.

16. On family trips, we all rode in the ___ seat.

17. It was a sad day when I had to ____ with my owls.

18. I still don't think Wol ever realized he was not a ____.

Pa Lia's First Day
Michelle Edwards

1. Pa Lia was very, very ____ about the first day at her new school.

2. Suddenly, she found herself all ____ in front of Jackson Magnet.

3. Jackson Magnet ____ just like the first day of school.

4. Someone yelled ____ ____. Pa Lia fell on the stairs and wanted to cry.

5. Pa Lia was rescued by a girl named ____.

6. She ____ Pa Lia to walk with her to their classroom.

7. There she introduced Pa Lia to her very best friend, ____.

8. Pa Lia felt nobody in the class wanted to be her ____.

9. Then she dreamed she could be part of a ____ of friends.

10. Instead of doing her math, Pa Lia drew two ____.

11. Each one showed a ____ nibbling a cookie.

12. She passed them to the two girls who ____ out loud.

13. Mrs. Fennessey demanded to know what was so ____.

14. In a shaky voice, Pa Lia ____ to the crime.

15. At recess, Pa Lia ____ out of the classroom.

16. She was sure what she had done was a ____ thing.

17. But the girls were proud she had told the ____.

18. After that, Jackson Magnet was no longer ____.

Paul Bunyan: A Tall Tale
Steven Kellogg

1. Paul Bunyan was born in the state of ____.

2. To handle him, Paul's parents anchored his ____ in the harbor.

3. Paul raced with the deer and wrestled with the ____.

4. Paul found a cold ox calf and named him ___.

5. When he was seventeen, Paul and his crew headed ___.

6. They were ambushed by ____ called Gumberoos.

7. They ran into a ____ that froze them for years.

8. Finally, spring could not wait any longer and ____.

9. While crossing Arizona, Paul's ax gouged the Grand ____.

10. Disaster struck but Paul beat it with a blizzard of ____.

11. They crossed California and reached the ____ Ocean.

12. Paul and Babe are said to be still roaming the ____ ranges.

Pinky and Rex
James Howe

1. Pinky and Rex lived across the ___ from each other.

2. Rex is going to the ____ with Pinky and his sister Amanda.

3. Pinky and Rex checked with each other about what ____ to wear.

4. Pinky loved to count his ____-____ beloved stuffed animals.

5. Rex's very special friends were her stuffed ____.

6. Amanda felt they should ____ some with her.

7. Pinky and Rex considered themselves very good ____.

8. At the museum, Pinky and Rex knew to save the ____ display for last.

9. So first they visited the new American ____ display.

10. At the wild animal display, the ____ was their favorite.

11. Pinky and Rex enjoyed the display of ____ and ores.

12. Amanda's only comment at each display was "____ ____?"

13. At the gift shop, all three children ____ the same thing.

14. Individually, they did not have enough ____.

15. Pinky and Rex together were short ____ cents.

16. Amanda added two quarters and the clerk said, "____."

17. Pinky and Rex share the ____ dinosaur for three days each.

18. And every ____, the dinosaur lives in Amanda's room.

Pippi Longstocking
Astrid Lindgren

1. ____ year old Pippi lived alone in an old house.

2. She came there after her father, a ship captain, was ____ at sea.

3. She brought Mr. Nilsson, a monkey, and a ____ of gold pieces with her.

4. Tommy and Annika were delighted to have Pippi living ____ ____.

5. For one thing, Pippi showed them how to be a ____ finder.

6. Pippi's one and only experience at ____ was rather a disaster.

7. The children had a secret hiding place in the ____ of an old tree.

8. Pippi's performance at the circus impressed all but the ____.

9. After that, everybody in town but two tramps knew of Pippi's ____.

10. The tramps spied her ____ her gold pieces.

11. They decided to ____ the gold when Pippi went to bed.

12. But it did not work out the way they ____.

13. Pippi's invitation to a ___ was another disaster.

14. Pippi rescued two children through the use of a ____.

15. Tommy and Annika went to Pippi's ____ party.

16. Their ____ to Pippi was a music box.

17. After refreshments, they had an unusual round of ____.

18. Pippi ended the evening in her ____ nightshirt.

Prairie School
Avi

1. Nine-year-old Noah and his parents lived in a ____ ____.

2. Aunt Dora was invited to teach Noah to ____ ____ ____.

3. Noah believed ____ was useless on the prairie.

4. Aunt Dora arrived with her ____.

5. For days, Noah used his ____ as an excuse to get out of lessons.

6. Aunt Dora asked Noah to push her around ____.

7. She looked up interesting flowers and bulbs that she saw in a ____.

8. At night she showed him how to read the ____.

9. Noah's first book was called a ____.

10. By the end of a week, Noah could recite the ____.

11. Noah could not get enough ____.

12. Daily, they ____ the prairie with their books.

13. Noah read to the family every ____.

14. Noah's parents were bursting with ____.

15. Noah ____ his mind about schooling and the prairie.

16. After Aunt Dora left, she and Noah ____ each other.

The Puppy Who Wanted a Boy
Jane Thayer

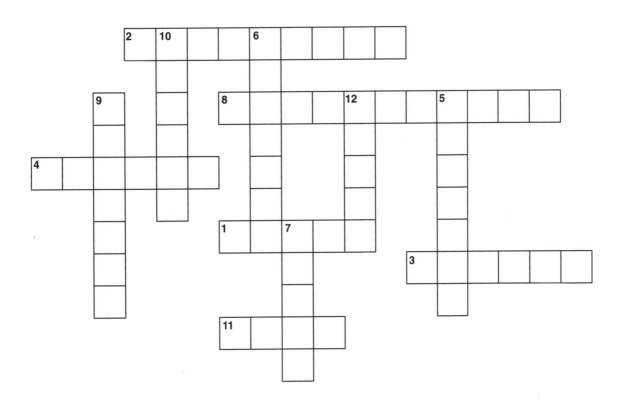

1. The main character is a puppy named ____.

2. The puppy wanted a boy for ____.

3. The puppy asked a ____ if he would give his boy away.

4. Then he asked a ____ if he would give his boy away.

5. The ____ would not give his boy away either.

6. Nor would the ____ give his boy away.

7. The puppy became very ____ and discouraged.

8. The puppy saw a sign that said ____ ____ ____.

9. He saw a little boy ____ all alone on the steps.

10. The puppy and the little boy ____ each other.

11. All the boys wanted to ____ the puppy.

12. That little puppy found ____ boys for Christmas.

Robert the Rose Horse
Joan Heilbroner

1. Robert lived on a ___ with his parents.

2. On his birthday, his friends came to his ____.

3. The birthday ____ was very pretty.

4. It was decorated with lots of real red ____.

5. When Robert sniffed, he gave a huge ____.

6. The doctor said Robert was ____ to the flowers.

7. Robert had to leave and find a job in the ____.

8. Robert found work driving the ____ ____ and his wagon.

9. Robert was happy until he got that ____ feeling.

10. Next Robert worked for a riding ____.

11. All was fine until his nose began to ____.

12. Finally he got a job as a ____ horse.

13. Three men with a ____ bag went into the bank.

14. Robert heard the alarm and saw the ____.

15. A flower helped Robert stop the bad guys ____.

16. After that Robert was all ____ out.

Sable
Karen Hesse

1. She was just a stray but she was the dog I ____.

2. Because she had the ____ fur, I named her Sable.

3. Pa builds ____ for people who live in cities.

4. In the worst way, I wanted Sable to ____ to me.

5. Mam hated dogs due to a bad ____.

6. I even took Sable to my special ____ place.

7. What I called Sable bringing home presents, Mam called ____.

8. Even when ____, Sable managed to free herself.

9. I could not believe it when Pap ____ Sable away to Doc Winston.

10. There was no way I could possibly live ____ Sable.

11. I decided to build a ____ like the one Doc Winston had.

12. Finally, after much work, my project was ____.

13. Mam and Pap agreed to let me go ____ Sable.

14. Mr. Cobb said he would let me ____ to Concord with him.

15. But I was really going to ____ my dog.

16. Doc Winston told me Sable had ____ ____ from his house.

17. Later, Mr. Cobb ____ Sable trying to get back to me.

18. Today, Pap and even Mam ____ Sable as much as I do.

Shrek!
William Steig

1. Shrek was _____ than his parents put together.

2. The day came when Shrek had to leave his black _____ of a home.

3. A witch foretold that he would wed a _____.

4. The magic words for this to happen were _____ strudel.

5. Everywhere Shrek went every kind of creature _____.

6. Even the thunder, lightning and rain _____.

7. Upon seeing it, Shrek ignored a _____ nailed to a tree.

8. He got the best of a poor _____ with a blue flame.

9. Shrek was disturbed in his sleep by a very _____ dream.

10. Then he tried the witch's magic words on a _____.

11. The words worked and Shrek rode to the _____.

12. A _____ in a suit of armor tried to stop him.

13. Instead Shrek stopped him with a _____ of fire.

14. Inside the castle Shrek felt _____ for the first time.

15. Then he discovered he was in the Hall of _____.

16. At last he said the magic words to his would-be _____.

17. She answered him with a coo, "_____-_____-_____."

18. They got married and lived _____ ever after.

The Sign Painter's Dream
Roger Roth

1. Everyone called him _____ Clarence.

2. His companion was a cat named _____.

3. Clarence complained that painting signs was _____.

4. He refused to paint Aunt Tillie a free sign for free _____.

5. Clarence had a dream visit from _____ Washington.

6. The general needed a sign painted for _____.

7. Clarence spent the whole night actually _____ his work.

8. In the morning, he drove to Aunt Tillie's _____.

9. Clarence set up a magnificent _____.

10. Aunt Tillie called him a real _____.

11. She served him a piece of _____ apple pie.

12. Clarence is now a very _____ man.

Stellaluna
Janell Cannon

1. Stellaluna and Mother _____ lived in the forest.

2. One night they were attacked by an _____.

3. Stellaluna escaped but fell into a bird _____.

4. She became so hungry, she finally had to eat _____.

5. She promised Mother Bird she would _____ the house rules.

6. Around the birds, Stellaluna felt she was very _____.

7. One day she became _____ from the birds.

8. She fell asleep hanging by her _____.

9. A large _____ of bats found her.

10. One of the bats turned out to be her _____.

11. Stellaluna was so happy to be back with her own _____.

12. Birds and bats are different but they can be _____.

The Story About Ping
Marjorie Flack

1. Ping lived in the country of ____.

2. Ping's home was a boat on the Yangtze ____.

3. At sunrise, Ping and his __ left the boat to find food.

4. At sunset, the Master ____ La La La La La Lei.

5. The ducks ____ back onto the boat.

6. The last duck always got a ____ on the back.

7. One day, Ping knew he would be last so he ____.

8. The next day, Ping could not find the ____ ____ boat.

9. He was captured by a boy whose mother planned to ____ him.

10. As the sun set the boy ____ Ping into the river.

11. Ping found the boat but he was ____ again.

12. Ping marched back onto the boat ____.

Strega Nona
Tomie de Paola

1. Strega Nona helped everyone through her magic ____.

2. She hired Big Anthony to be her ____.

3. Strega Nona told him never to touch her ____ pot.

4. Big Anthony discovered the pot was ____.

5. A special chant caused the pot to ____ ____.

6. Big Anthony blabbed but nobody ____ him.

7. When Strega Nona was away he ____ it.

8. But he could not get the pot to ____.

9. Everyone was almost ____ in pasta.

10. Strega Nona returned and ____ the day.

11. She made Big Anthony ____ all the pasta.

12. All because Big Anthony did not blow ____ kisses.

The Tortoise and the Jackrabbit
Susan Lowell

1. It was springtime in the ____.

2. Old Tortoise challenged Jackrabbit to a ____.

3. Tortoise ____ from the starting line.

4. Jackrabbit ____ from the starting line.

5. Jackrabbit was soon so far ahead he stopped for a ____.

6. Tortoise finally reached the ____ flat place.

7. Tortoise passed Jackrabbit sleeping under the ____ trees.

8. All of a sudden, Jackrabbit ____ ____.

9. Tortoise was very close to the ____ line.

10. Jackrabbit raced to ____ Tortoise.

11. He crashed right into ____.

12. Tortoise ____ her point and won the race.

Tortoise Brings the Mail
Dee Lillegard

1. Tortoise's job was to deliver ____.

2. But everyone complained he was too ____.

3. When Crow boasted he was __, he got the job.

4. But in his hurry, he ____ most of the mail.

5. Tortoise ____ took his old job back.

6. Rabbit boasted he could do ____ than Tortoise or Crow.

7. But Rabbit delivered the mail to the wrong ____.

8. Tortoise hummed and smiled as he ____ the mail again.

9. Fox bragged he never made ____.

10. But Fox was ____ all the interesting packages.

11. Tortoise offered to help him but Fox got scared and left the ___.

12. Tortoise hummed and smiled for Tortoise ____ his job.

Tree of Birds
Susan Meddaugh

1. Harry only heard the _____ that hit the bird's wing.

2. He took her _____ to care for her and named her Sally.

3. Harry's library book told him Sally was a _____ tufted tropical.

4. Sally healed but she seemed sad and had no _____.

5. Harry became aware of a strange feeling of being _____.

6. He discovered a _____ full of birds just like Sally.

7. The birds followed Harry _____ he went.

8. _____ was here but the birds would not fly south.

9. Harry was worried. A big _____ was coming.

10. Sally _____ the birds from Harry's bedroom window.

11. Harry opened the window for Sally to fly away with her _____.

12. Instead, all the birds joined Sally in Harry's _____.

Verdi
Janell Cannon

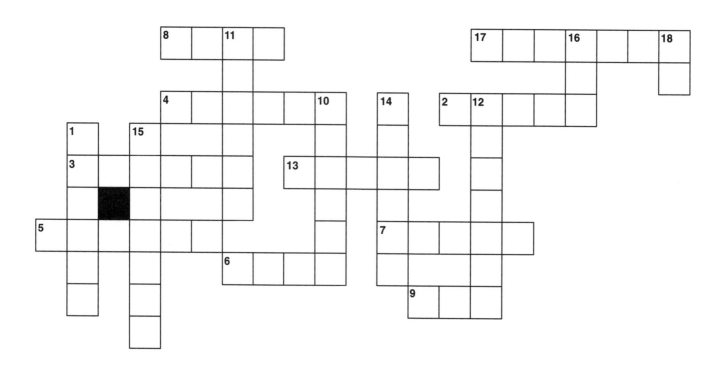

1. Mother ____ sent her hatchlings into the forest.

2. She told them to grow up big and ____.

3. But Verdi liked his ____ skin.

4. He thought the greens were dull and ____.

5. He decided he would move too fast to ____.

6. But one day his ____ began to peel.

7. He decided to ____ the stripe off.

8. Verdi's actions caught the eye of a large ___.

9. He escaped but was covered with ____.

10. He sailed off a tree hoping the sun would turn him ____.

11. He landed very hard in a crooked ____.

12. The greens ____ him and gave him first aid.

13. They shared with him their days of ____ and adventure.

14. When Verdi was healed he listened to the ____.

15. He became content as he ___ with the leaves.

16. Two young yellow snakes made ____ of Verdi.

17. Verdi proved he could still ____.

18. Then he told the little greens, "I am still ____."

Answers

Abigail Takes the Wheel

1. Neptune
2. New York City
3. school
4. collided
5. tow
6. wheel
7. steer
8. first mate
9. charge
10. Hudson
11. Bristol
12. reverse
13. forty two
14. whistle
15. crashing
16. tired
17. crews
18. saluted

The Adventures of Captain Underpants

1. practical
2. superheroes
3. coolest
4. school
5. hated
6. video
7. forced
8. catering
9. hyporing
10. spell
11. obeys
12. secret
13. real
14. robots
15. evil
16. plastic
17. finally
18. snapping

Agapanthus Hum and the Eyeglasses

1. humming
2. glasses
3. sat
4. mend
5. encouraged
6. paper bag
7. pocket
8. acrobats
9. clown
10. strawberry
11. famous

12. clean
13. water
14. lopsided
15. star
16. washed
17. mother
18. best

Amber Brown Is Not a Crayon

1. preschool
2. China
3. teasing
4. fortune
5. Alabama
6. sells
7. true
8. airplane
9. weeks
10. chewing gum
11. friend
12. unbaked
13. speaking
14. without
15. going away
16. leaving
17. meet
18. third

Amelia Bedelia

1. chores
2. lemon
3. change
4. dust
5. drapes
6. lights
7. measure
8. steak
9. dress
10. fire
11. loved
12. learned

Amos and Boris

1. mouse
2. travel
3. Rodent
4. loved
5. rolled
6. whale
7. friends
8. Africa
9. hurricane
10. recognized
11. elephants

12. forget

Annabel the Actress Starring in Just a Little Extra

1. break
2. movie
3. actress
4. extras
5. crowd
6. noticed
7. Winona
8. part
9. scream
10. waiting
11. show
12. flip flops
13. Cut. Print it!
14. believe
15. four
16. close up
17. gray green
18. thank you

Arthur's Computer Disaster

1. computer
2. Dark
3. greatest
4. thing
5. office
6. orders
7. demands
8. keyboard
9. screen
10. fix it
11. Brain
12. worried
13. admitted
14. switch
15. week
16. good night
17. hooked
18. series

Babar Loses His Crown

1. Paris
2. crown
3. wrong
4. mustache
5. find
6. Eiffel
7. bridge
8. false
9. subway
10. hotel

11. opera
12. king
13. bumps
14. red
15. flute
16. great

A Bargain for Frances

1. friend
2. problems
3. best
4. saving
5. plastic
6. buying
7. china
8. penny
9. backsies
10. tricks
11. money
12. exchange
13. happy
14. careful
15. share
16. lesson

Beans Baker, Number Five

1. uniforms
2. twenty one
3. believe
4. Wrong Way
5. quit
6. change
7. practice
8. ready
9. two
10. ninth
11. swaggered
12. fainted
13. bat
14. strikes
15. home
16. number

Beezus and Ramona

1. exasperating
2. imagination
3. rabbit
4. bad
5. bite
6. birthday
7. aunt
8. party
9. mother
10. parade
11. age
12. perfect
13. tricks
14. batter
15. smelled

16. Gretel
17. saved
18. time

Betsy-Tacy

1. fifth
2. piano
3. bashful
4. Betsy
5. Bee
6. sand
7. nickels
8. play
9. once
10. chocolate
11. imagination
12. sister
13. family
14. comforted
15. summer
16. Tib
17. similar
18. marries

Big Max

1. Pooka
2. elephant
3. umbrella
4. gold
5. clues
6. stolen
7. ice
8. tracks
9. crocodile
10. noise
11. party
12. family
13. solved
14. cakes
15. melted
16. chocolate

The Boxcar Children

1. four
2. grandfather
3. sleep
4. ran away
5. boxcar
6. thorn
7. dump
8. odd jobs
9. swimming
10. cherries
11. paper
12. rich
13. field
14. free for all
15. Violet
16. home

17. figured
18. beautiful

Breakout at the Bug Lab

1. mom
2. cockroach
3. Nature
4. party
5. dog
6. missing
7. ceiling
8. scream
9. lady
10. rubber
11. Oneshot
12. ping
13. tank
14. ribbon
15. news
16. told

Buford the Little Bighorn

1. horns
2. friends
3. valley
4. hideout
5. hunting
6. plane
7. mountains
8. trail
9. skis
10. snow
11. resort
12. star

Cam Jansen and the Mystery of the Dinosaur Bones

1. photographic
2. the camera
3. click
4. museum
5. dinosaur
6. three
7. would not
8. postcards
9. guard
10. brand
11. guide
12. discover
13. whistles
14. escaped
15. fired
16. mystery

The Camel Who Took a Walk

1. between
2. hidden
3. beautiful
4. shadow

5. coconut
6. unaware
7. bite
8. bird
9. reached
10. ready
11. yawn
12. nothing

Caps for Sale

1. peddler
2. head
3. Fifty
4. sell
5. walk
6. sleep
7. missing
8. monkey
9. return
10. ground
11. flying
12. checked
13. town
14. balance

The Captain Contest

1. summer
2. problem
3. decided
4. leader
5. cheetah
6. first
7. person
8. better
9. compete
10. decision
11. friend
12. idea
13. okay
14. coach
15. one
16. Dewey
17. Bundy
18. Soccer

The Case of the Puzzling Possum

1. brains
2. snoop
3. button
4. trombone
5. clues
6. muddy
7. hayride
8. Mr. Riley
9. thirty
10. possum
11. follow
12. fun
13. music

14. guilty
15. plan
16. cleans

Charlotte's Web

1. runt
2. Homer
3. friend
4. voice
5. spider
6. daily
7. rat
8. smoked
9. save
10. worried
11. rotten
12. magic
13. miracle
14. message
15. mother
16. time
17. life
18. magnum opus

The Chocolate Touch

1. candy
2. chocolate
3. nose
4. harm
5. unusual
6. spent
7. golden
8. tasted
9. changed
10. trumpet
11. water
12. empty
13. elixir
14. disease
15. kissed
16. reappeared
17. window
18. normal

Click, Clack, Moo: Cows That Type

1. problem
2. found
3. typed
4. communicate
5. electric
6. strike
7. Sorry
8. hens
9. Closed
10. demanded
11. Duck
12. snoop
13. answer
14. exchange

15. agreed
16. diving board

Clifford the Big Red Dog

1. Elizabeth
2. reddest
3. ride
4. games
5. mistakes
6. habits
7. cats
8. drink
9. watchdog
10. bother
11. prize
12. trade

Cloudy with a Chance of Meatballs

1. Grandpa
2. swallow
3. sky
4. weather
5. hamburgers
6. spaghetti
7. enormous
8. handle
9. abandon
10. bread
11. supermarket
12. butter

Corduroy

1. bear
2. toy
3. buy
4. wanted
5. button
6. green
7. escalator
8. crash
9. night
10. shelf
11. Lisa
12. piggy bank
13. bed
14. fixed
15. home
16. friend

Curious George

1. monkey
2. Africa
3. yellow hat
4. telephone
5. fire station
6. prison
7. escaped
8. red

9. sailed
10. traffic
11. rescued
12. zoo

Dance with Rosie

1. ballet
2. grandmother
3. friends
4. together
5. date
6. syrup
7. window
8. sneaked
9. class
10. disaster
11. fighting
12. crows
13. Jenny
14. dancer
15. heads
16. place
17. made up
18. Rosaleen

Danny and the Dinosaur Go to Camp

1. camp
2. vacation
3. wins
4. ketchup
5. pizza
6. hiking
7. room
8. bunk
9. pillow
10. first

Dinosaurs Before Dark

1. before
2. books
3. reptile
4. spinning
5. oak
6. Henry
7. gold
8. dinosaurs
9. tyrannosaurus
10. pack
11. between
12. climbed
13. rope
14. wish
15. time
16. magic
17. tomorrow
18. first

Don't Fidget a Feather!

1. competing
2. champion
3. freeze
4. bee
5. bunnies
6. crows
7. wind
8. fox
9. stew
10. chosen
11. Duck
12. vegetable

Elmer

1. elephants
2. patchwork
3. happy
4. slipped
5. berries
6. gray
7. recognize
8. Booo
9. rain
10. celebrate
11. color
12. ordinary

Emma's Magic Winter

1. reading
2. neighbor
3. door
4. red
5. magic
6. lunch
7. other
8. brother
9. read
10. easy
11. snow
12. Speak
13. first
14. whisper
15. idea
16. voice
17. played
18. ropes

The Five Chinese Brothers

1. mother
2. swallow
3. iron
4. stretch
5. burned
6. breath
7. fishing
8. obey
9. drowned
10. arrested
11. another
12. innocent

A Flea in the Ear

1. spotted
2. wily
3. Stay away
4. ducks
5. flea
6. secret
7. accepted
8. drown
9. deal
10. stole
11. tricked
12. home

Franklin Fibs

1. things
2. seventy
3. fibbed
4. boasted
5. bragged
6. crowed
7. admitted
8. imagination
9. dared
10. excuses
11. truth
12. blink
13. entire
14. gulp
15. lesson
16. turtle

Freckle Juice

1. problems
2. Nickys
3. secret
4. fifty
5. piggy bank
6. buying
7. three
8. mixed
9. happen
10. stomach
11. blue
12. laughed
13. removing
14. hated
15. special
16. frog

Frederick

1. chatty
2. winter
3. sun rays
4. colors
5. words

6. supplies
7. hungry
8. share
9. warmer
10. minds
11. seasons
12. poet

Frog and Toad Together

1. chapter
2. list
3. crossed
4. blew
5. sleep
6. seeds
7. grow
8. ready
9. cookies
10. birds
11. bravery
12. afraid
13. together
14. dream
15. smaller
16. happy
17. friends

George the Drummer Boy

1. Boston
2. England
3. taxes
4. Concord
5. training
6. questions
7. Charles
8. Fred
9. two
10. minute men
11. battle
12. surrounded
13. fire
14. shot
15. escape
16. Revolution

Gertrude, the Bulldog Detective

1. mystery
2. detective
3. snooping
4. gang
5. museum
6. bundle
7. kidnappers
8. Rialto
9. police
10. sewed
11. ruby urn
12. knew

The Hallo-Wiener

1. different
2. Halloween
3. hot dog
4. feelings
5. wiener
6. treats
7. monster
8. pond
9. cats
10. life raft
11. shared
12. hero

The Hamster Chase

1. four
2. hamster
3. sneezes
4. classroom
5. computers
6. chew
7. closet
8. food
9. sunflower
10. floor
11. nose
12. books
13. nibbles
14. achoo
15. fur
16. Keats

Harry the Dirty Dog

1. black
2. baths
3. ran away
4. dirty
5. white
6. home
7. recognize
8. scrubbing
9. bathtub
10. begged
11. Harry
12. pillow

Henry and Mudge

1. child
2. friends
3. agreed
4. special
5. collars
6. worry
7. happily
8. loved
9. sleep
10. without
11. lost
12. cried

13. leave
14. called
15. found
16. dreams
17. always
18. series

Herbie Jones

1. apples
2. postcard
3. Annabelle
4. salmon
5. haunted
6. rescued
7. reading
8. spiders
9. partners
10. cheeseburgers
11. spanking
12. Donuts
13. vacuumed
14. murder
15. explained
16. changed

Hot-Air Henry

1. turn
2. cat
3. solo
4. stow away
5. sailed
6. drifted
7. down
8. air
9. blackbirds
10. eagle
11. Colson Hill
12. purrmewed

How Do Dinosaurs Say Good Night?

1. goodnight
2. tail
3. teddy
4. book
5. roar
6. Mama
7. swing
8. piggyback
9. tricks
10. kiss
11. light
12. tucks
13. whisper
14. hug

How to Make an Apple Pie and See the World

1. travel

2. Italy
3. chicken
4. cinnamon
5. English
6. water
7. sugarcane
8. apples
9. ingredients
10. friends
11. Vanilla
12. plain

Hugo and the Bully Frogs

1. croak
2. picked
3. fight
4. friendly
5. advice
6. I can't
7. No pushing
8. Quack
9. bellowed
10. surrounded
11. scared
12. happy

The Hundred Dresses

1. picking
2. dresses
3. different
4. Boggins
5. noticed
6. hundred
7. target
8. designing
9. motorboats
10. winner
11. displayed
12. moving
13. house
14. letter
15. give
16. drawn

Ira Sleeps Over

1. sleep
2. problem
3. teddy bear
4. silly
5. without
6. worried
7. laugh
8. agree
9. opinion
10. packed
11. bedroom
12. ghost
13. scared
14. drawer

15. Foo Foo
16. home
17. sound
18. Tah Tah

The Island of the Skog

1. Rodent
2. cat
3. island
4. Bouncer
5. North
6. Skog
7. monster
8. cannonballs
9. trap
10. flapping
11. animal
12. village

Jack and the Beanstalk

1. adventure
2. Daisy
3. magic
4. window
5. enormous
6. castle
7. agreed
8. hide
9. Fee fi fo fum
10. golden
11. rope
12. lowered
13. harp
14. chase
15. break
16. might
17. catapulted
18. ever after

The Joy Boys

1. cows
2. shouted
3. bull
4. under
5. shoes
6. mud bombs
7. moving
8. mad
9. fighting
10. real
11. sorry
12. wild
13. scared
14. sleeping
15. nose
16. between

Julian's Glorious Summer

1. makes up

2. Gloria
3. problem
4. lied
5. father
6. hates
7. working
8. Huey
9. money
10. bicycle
11. return
12. fall
13. hurting
14. cement
15. balance
16. proud
17. pedal
18. exploring

Katy and the Big Snow

1. tractor
2. snow plow
3. nothing
4. storm
5. big snow
6. stopped
7. Follow me
8. down
9. east
10. hospital
11. fire
12. airport
13. home
14. rest

Katy No-Pocket

1. Kangaroo
2. pocket
3. animals
4. back
5. arms
6. don't
7. city
8. apron
9. neck
10. faster
11. babysitter
12. world

King Emmett the Second

1. Ohio
2. refuse
3. pig
4. dead
5. acres
6. bad
7. friends
8. bicycle
9. training
10. removes

11. falling
12. steady
13. Cruz
14. likes
15. birthday
16. pets
17. dog
18. King

The Legend of the Bluebonnet: An Old Tale of Texas

1. drought
2. healing
3. warrior
4. sacrifice
5. valued
6. willing
7. spirits
8. night
9. burned
10. scattered
11. blue
12. forgiveness

The Legend of the Indian Paintbrush

1. Gopher
2. strength
3. decorate
4. special
5. vision
6. tools
7. buckskin
8. setting
9. pictures
10. remember
11. colors
12. brushes
13. painted
14. flowers

The Librarian from the Black Lagoon

1. library
2. boiler
3. Beamster
4. Igor
5. steps
6. bolted
7. catalog
8. Dewey
9. overdue
10. Congress
11. mouse
12. joke
13. happy
14. welcome
15. smiles
16. love

17. teasing
18. wacky

Little Bear

1. four
2. winter
3. snow
4. fur
5. birthday
6. soup
7. friends
8. cake
9. moon
10. lunch
11. little
12. home
13. Earth
14. sleep
15. wishes
16. story
17. himself
18. animal

Little House in the Big Woods

1. Wisconsin
2. grocery
3. winter
4. work
5. stories
6. safe
7. Christmas
8. Sunday
9. maple sugar
10. shoes
11. town
12. happy
13. hair
14. honey
15. harvest
16. threshers
17. settled
18. authors

Little Pear: The Story of a Little Chinese Boy

1. China
2. highway
3. river
4. five
5. walking
6. shoulders
7. cart
8. lesson
9. New Years
10. firecrackers
11. kites
12. flew away
13. peaches

14. freedom
15. fair
16. fell
17. family
18. promised

Little Rabbit's Loose Tooth

1. first
2. soft
3. other
4. chocolate
5. window
6. bath
7. thought
8. fairy
9. pillow
10. tooth
11. ready
12. check
13. dime
14. your

Little Toot

1. whistle
2. tugboats
3. playing
4. sissy
5. tide
6. waves
7. rocket
8. ocean
9. SOS
10. rescue
11. headway
12. green
13. bounced
14. line
15. pulled
16. hero
17. best
18. adventures

Little Whistle

1. Toytown
2. guinea pig
3. sleeping
4. pea coat
5. adventure
6. something
7. hollow log
8. home
9. friends
10. different
11. shades
12. visit
13. activities
14. sold
15. live
16. content

17. reader
18. warm

Madeline

1. Paris
2. Twelve
3. smiled
4. nine
5. smallest
6. frighten
7. sick
8. appendix
9. hospital
10. better
11. scar
12. wrong
13. crying
14. wanted
15. well
16. series

Mary Moon Is Missing

1. race
2. message
3. family
4. body
5. engaged
6. solve
7. wrist
8. stuffed
9. purple
10. bridge
11. Mischief
12. steal
13. trouble
14. rock
15. washed
16. Cafe
17. locked
18. thief
19. cold
20. arrest

Mike Mulligan and His Steam Shovel

1. Mary Anne
2. team
3. hundred
4. work
5. Popperville
6. day
7. nothing
8. sun up
9. finished
10. forgotten
11. furnace
12. janitor

Ming Lo Moves the Mountain

1. bottom
2. unhappiness
3. move
4. tree
5. noise
6. spirit
7. smoke
8. dance
9. bundles
10. closed
11. far
12. did not

Miss Nelson Is Missing!

1. worst
2. teacher
3. substitute
4. Swamp
5. witch
6. work
7. terrible
8. police
9. unhappy
10. returned
11. behaved
12. secret

Miss Rumphius

1. Alice
2. faraway
3. beautiful
4. library
5. world
6. camel
7. sea
8. lupine
9. patch
10. scattering
11. three
12. great aunt

The Mitten

1. wool
2. Baba
3. dropped
4. mole
5. rabbit
6. prickles
7. owl
8. badger
9. muzzle
10. nosed
11. fast
12. mouse
13. sneezed
14. home
15. window
16. sound

17. mitttens
18. large

Morris and Boris

1. three
2. riddles
3. answers
4. really
5. home
6. twisters
7. understand
8. argument
9. away
10. bird
11. games
12. seek
13. way
14. angry
15. bear
16. moose

The Mouse and the Motorcycle

1. knot hole
2. days
3. red
4. wastebasket
5. peered
6. talk
7. noise
8. speeding
9. promised
10. maid
11. leave
12. crash
13. confess
14. friends
15. fever
16. aspirin
17. ambulance
18. gave

A Mouse Called Wolf

1. important
2. teased
3. piano
4. melodies
5. sing
6. voice
7. cat
8. ballad
9. music
10. chocolates
11. together
12. come
13. courage
14. ankle
15. window
16. composed

Muggie Maggie

1. writing
2. contrary
3. loops
4. computer
5. conference
6. motivated
7. ready
8. back
9. talked
10. signed
11. Muggie
12. ballpoint
13. printed
14. read
15. delivered
16. name
17. practiced
18. wanted

My Father's Dragon

1. three
2. cat
3. ferry
4. save
5. stowaway
6. rocks
7. invaded
8. peels
9. sensed
10. chewing
11. paste
12. lion
13. boars
14. gorilla
15. magnifying
16. lollipops
17. hurry
18. jackknife
19. All aboard
20. return

Nate the Great

1. alone
2. picture
3. Sherlock
4. yellow
5. dog
6. buried
7. friend
8. innocent
9. brother
10. suspicious
11. color
12. orange
13. solved
14. monster

15. endings
16. series

Owen Foote, Second Grade Strongman

1. small
2. pipsqueak
3. strongman
4. gran
5. size
6. almost
7. bully
8. principals
9. seventh
10. manners
11. office
12. nice
13. hearing
14. bloomer
15. answer
16. secret
17. character
18. success

Owls in the Family

1. Canada
2. owls nest
3. pets
4. young
5. brush
6. friend
7. cage
8. scout
9. fly
10. safety
11. crossed
12. rattlesnake
13. jokes
14. skunk
15. scream
16. rumble
17. part
18. human

Pa Lia's First Day

1. nervous
2. alone
3. smelled
4. four eyes
5. Calliope
6. invited
7. Howie
8. friend
9. trio
10. pictures
11. mouse
12. laughed
13. funny

14. confessed
15. raced
16. stinker
17. truth
18. scary

Paul Bunyan: A Tall Tale

1. Maine
2. cradle
3. grizzlies
4. Babe
5. west
6. ogres
7. blizzard
8. exploded
9. Canyon
10. popcorn
11. Pacific
12. Alaskan

Pinky and Rex

1. street
2. museum
3. outfits
4. twenty seven
5. dinosaurs
6. share
7. friends
8. best
9. Indian
10. bobcat
11. minerals
12. Who cares
13. wanted
14. money
15. fifty
16. Sold
17. pink
18. Sunday

Pippi Longstocking

1. Nine
2. lost
3. suitcase
4. next door
5. thing
6. school
7. hollow
8. ringmaster
9. strength
10. counting
11. steal
12. planned
13. coffee
14. rope
15. birthday
16. gift
17. games

18. fathers

Prairie School

1. sod house
2. read and write
3. schooling
4. wheelchair
5. chores
6. outdoors
7. book
8. sky
9. primer
10. alphabet
11. reading
12. explored
13. evening
14. pride
15. changed
16. wrote

The Puppy Who Wanted a Boy

1. Petey
2. Christmas
3. collie
4. setter
5. bulldog
6. scottie
7. tired
8. home for boys
9. sitting
10. hugged
11. keep
12. fifty

Robert the Rose Horse

1. farm
2. party
3. cake
4. roses
5. kerchoo
6. allergic
7. city
8. milk man
9. funny
10. stable
11. itch
12. police
13. black
14. robbers
15. flat
16. sneezed

Sable

1. wanted
2. softest
3. furniture
4. belong
5. experience
6. secret

7. stealing
8. chained
9. gave
10. without
11. fence
12. finished
13. visit
14. drive
15. fetch
16. run off
17. found
18. love

Shrek!

1. uglier
2. hole
3. princess
4. apple
5. fled
6. departed
7. sign
8. dragon
9. bad
10. donkey
11. castle
12. knight
13. blast
14. fear
15. Mirrors
16. bride
17. cock a doodle
18. horribly

The Sign Painter's Dream

1. Crabby
2. Amanda
3. boring
4. apples
5. General
6. free
7. enjoying
8. orchard
9. sign
10. hero
11. perfect
12. happy

Stellaluna

1. Bat
2. owl
3. nest
4. bugs
5. obey
6. clumsy
7. separated
8. thumbs
9. group
10. mother
11. family

12. friends

The Story About Ping

1. China
2. River
3. family
4. called
5. marched
6. spank
7. hid
8. wise eyed
9. cook
10. dropped
11. late
12. anyway

Strega Nona

1. touch
2. helper
3. pasta
4. magic
5. fill up
6. believed
7. proved
8. stop
9. buried
10. saved
11. eat
12. three

The Tortoise and the Jackrabbit

1. desert
2. race
3. trudged
4. bolted
5. snooze
6. dusty
7. mesquite
8. woke up
9. finish
10. catch
11. coyote
12. proved

Tortoise Brings the Mail

1. mail
2. slow
3. faster
4. dropped
5. happily
6. better
7. mailboxes
8. delivered
9. mistakes
10. stealing
11. forest
12. loved

Tree of Birds

1. car
2. home
3. green
4. appetite
5. followed
6. tree
7. everywhere
8. Winter
9. snowstorm
10. watched
11. friends
12. room

Verdi

1. python
2. green
3. yellow
4. boring
5. change
6. skin
7. scrub
8. fish
9. mud
10. golden
11. sprawl
12. rescued
13. glory
14. forest
15. blended
16. fun
17. perform
18. me

Bibliography

Abigail Takes the Wheel by Avi. HarperCollins, 2000.

The Adventures of Captain Underpants by Dav Pilkey. Scholastic, 1997.

Agapanthus Hum and the Eyeglasses by Joy Cowley. Penguin Putnam, 2001.

Amber Brown Is Not a Crayon by Paula Danziger. Scholastic, 1995.

Amelia Bedelia by Peggy Parish. HarperCollins, 1999.

Amos and Boris by William Steig. Farrar, Straus and Giroux, 1992.

Annabel the Actress Starring in Just a Little Extra by Ellen Conford. Simon & Schuster, 2001.

Arthur's Computer Disaster by Marc Brown. Little, Brown and Company, 1999.

Babar Loses His Crown by Laurent de Brunhoff. Beginner Books, 1976.

A Bargain for Frances by Russell Hoban. HarperCollins, 1978.

Beans Baker, Number Five by Richard Torrey. Golden Books, 2001.

Beezus and Ramona by Beverly Cleary. HarperCollins, 1990.

Betsy-Tacy by Maud Hart Lovelace. HarperCollins, 1994.

Big Max by Kin Platt. HarperCollins, 1991.

The Boxcar Children by Gertrude Chandler Warner. Albert Whitman, 2002.

Breakout at the Bug Lab by Ruth Horowitz. Penguin Putnam, 2002.

Buford the Little Bighorn by Bill Peet. Houghton Mifflin, 1983.

Cam Jansen and the Mystery of the Dinosaur Bones by David Adler. Viking Penguin, 1997.

The Camel Who Took a Walk by Jack Tworkov. Dutton Children's Books, 1991.

Caps for Sale by Esphyr Slobodkina. HarperCollins, 1987.

The Captain Contest by Matt Christopher. Little, Brown and Company, 2001.

The Case of the Puzzling Possum by Cynthia Rylant. Greenwillow Books, 2001.

Charlotte's Web by E. B. White. HarperCollins, 2001.

The Chocolate Touch by Patrick Skene Catling. Bantam Doubleday Dell, 1996.

Click, Clack, Moo: Cows That Type by Doreen Cronin. Simon & Schuster, 2000.

Clifford the Big Red Dog by Norman Bridwell. Scholastic, 1990.

Cloudy with a Chance of Meatballs by Judi Barrett. Simon & Schuster, 1982.

Corduroy by Don Freeman. Penguin USA, 1976.

Curious George by H. A. Rey. Houghton Mifflin, 1973.

Dance with Rosie by Patricia Reilly Giff. Penguin Putnam, 1997.

Danny and the Dinosaur Go to Camp by Syd Hoff. HarperCollins, 1999.

Dinosaurs Before Dark by Mary Pope Osborne. Random House, 1992.

Don't Fidget a Feather! by Erica Silverman. Simon & Schuster, 1998.

Elmer by David McKee. William Morrow and Co., 1991.

Emma's Magic Winter by Jean Little. HarperCollins, 2000.

The Five Chinese Brothers by Claire Bishop. Putnam, 1998.

A Flea in the Ear by Stephen Wyllie. Penguin Putnam, 1996.

Franklin Fibs by Paulette Bourgeois. Scholastic, 1992.

Freckle Juice by Judy Blume. Bantam Doubleday Dell, 1978.

Frederick by Leo Lionni. Knopf, 1973.

Frog and Toad Together by Arnold Lobel. HarperCollins, 1979.

George the Drummer Boy by Nathaniel Benchley. HarperCollins, 1987.

Gertrude, the Bulldog Detective by Eileen Christelow. Random House, 1995.

The Hallo-Wiener by Dav Pilkey. Scholastic, 1999.

The Hamster Chase by Anastasia Suen. Penguin Putnam, 2002.

Harry the Dirty Dog by Gene Zion. HarperCollins, 1976.

Henry and Mudge by Cynthia Rylant. Simon & Schuster, 1996.

Herbie Jones by Suzy Kline. Penguin Putnam, 2002.

Hot-Air Henry by Mary Calhoun. William Morrow and Co., 1984.

How Do Dinosaurs Say Good Night? by Jane Yolen. Scholastic, 2000.

How to Make an Apple Pie and See the World by Marjorie Priceman. Bantam Doubleday Dell, 1996.

Hugo and the Bully Frogs by Francesca Simon. David & Charles Children's Books, 2000.

The Hundred Dresses by Eleanor Estes. Harcourt, 1991.

Ira Sleeps Over by Bernard Waber. Houghton Mifflin, 1975.

The Island of the Skog by Steven Kellogg. Penguin Putnam, 1976.

Jack and the Beanstalk by Richard Walker. Barefoot Books, 2002.

The Joy Boys by Betsy Byars. Bantam Doubleday Dell, 1996.

Julian's Glorious Summer by Ann Cameron. Random House, 1987.

Katy and the Big Snow by Virginia Lee Burton. Houghton Mifflin, 1974.

Katy No-Pocket by Emmy Payne. Houghton Mifflin, 1972.

King Emmett the Second by Mary Stolz. Random House, 1993.

The Legend of the Bluebonnet: An Old Tale of Texas by Tomie de Paola. Putnam, 1996.

The Legend of the Indian Paintbrush by Tomie de Paola. Putnam, 1991.

The Librarian from the Black Lagoon by Mike Thaler. Scholastic, 1997.

Little Bear by Else Minarik. HarperCollins, 1978.

Little House in the Big Woods by Laura Ingalls Wilder. HarperCollins, 1976.

Little Pear: The Story of a Little Chinese Boy by Eleanor Frances Lattimore. Harcourt, 1991.

Little Rabbit's Loose Tooth by Lucy Bate. Crown Books for Young Readers, 1983.

Little Toot by Hardie Gramatky. Penguin Putnam, 2000.

Little Whistle by Cynthia Rylant. Harcourt, 2001.

Madeline by Ludwig Bemelmans. Viking Penguin, 1976.

Mary Moon Is Missing by Patricia Reilly Giff. Penguin Putnam, 2000.

Mike Mulligan and His Steam Shovel by Virginia Lee Burton. Houghton Mifflin, 1977.

Ming Lo Moves the Mountain by Arnold Lobel. William Morrow and Co., 1993.

Miss Nelson Is Missing! by Harry Allard. Houghton Mifflin, 1985.

Miss Rumphius by Barbara Cooney. Penguin Putnam, 1985.

The Mitten by Jan Brett. Putnam, 1989.

Morris and Boris by Bernard Wiseman. Putnam, 1991.

The Mouse and the Motorcycle by Beverly Cleary. HarperCollins, 1990.

A Mouse Called Wolf by Dick King-Smith. Knopf, 1999.

Muggie Maggie by Beverly Cleary. HarperCollins, 1991.

My Father's Dragon by Ruth Stiles Gannett. Knopf, 1987.

Nate the Great by Marjorie Weinman Sharmat. Bantam Doubleday Dell, 1977.

Owen Foote, Second Grade Strongman by Stephanie Greene. Houghton Mifflin, 1996.

Owls in the Family by Farley Mowat. Bantam Doubleday Dell, 1981.

Pa Lia's First Day by Michelle Edwards. Harcourt, 2001.

Paul Bunyan: A Tall Tale by Steven Kellogg. William Morrow and Co., 1994.

Pinky and Rex by James Howe. Simon & Schuster, 1998.

Pippi Longstocking by Astrid Lindgren. Penguin Putnam, 1976.

Prairie School by Avi. HarperCollins, 2001.

The Puppy Who Wanted a Boy by Jane Thayer. William Morrow and Co., 1991.

Robert the Rose Horse by Joan Heilbroner. Random House, 1989.

Sable by Karen Hesse. Henry Holt and Co., 1998.

Shrek! by William Steig. Farrar, Straus and Giroux, 1993.

The Sign Painter's Dream by Roger Roth. Crown Books for Young Readers, 1995.

Stellaluna by Janell Cannon. Harcourt, 1993.

The Story About Ping by Marjorie Flack. Penguin Putnam, 2000.

Strega Nona by Tomie de Paola. Simon & Schuster, 1997.

The Tortoise and the Jackrabbit by Susan Lowell. Northland Publishing AZ, 1994.

Tortoise Brings the Mail by Dee Lillegard. Dutton Children's Books, 1997.

Tree of Birds by Susan Meddaugh. Houghton Mifflin, 1994.

Verdi by Janell Cannon. Harcourt, 1996.